THE OUTER GATE

Photograph by Arnold Genthe.

THE OUTER GATE

THE COLLECTED POEMS OF NORA MAY FRENCH

Edited by Donald Sidney-Fryer and Alan Gullette

Hippocampus Press

New York

Copyright © 1910 by the Strange Company
Copyright © 2009 by Donald Sidney-Fryer and Alan Gullette

Originally edited by Henry Anderson Lafler, George Sterling, and Porter Garnett. Re-edited by Donald Sidney-Fryer and Alan Gullette.

"Thy Spirit Walks the Sea," by Donald Sidney-Fryer, *Songs and Sonnets Atlantean*, Arkham House, Sauk City, Wisconsin, 1971. Copyright © 1971 by Donald Sidney-Fryer.

". . . to secret places," by Dorothy Jesse Beagle, *Nora May French: Her Poems*, Star Rover House, Oakland, 1986. Copyright © 1986 by Dorothy Jesse Beagle.

"For Nora May in Paradise," by Mary Rudge, an original poem expressly revised and completed for this appearance. Copyright © 2007 by Mary Rudge.

"Nora May," by Alan Gullette, an original poem expressly written for this volume. Copyright © 2007 by Alan Gullette.

"For Nora May French," by Valerie Beatts, an original poem expressly written for this volume. Copyright © 2007 by Valerie Beatts.

"Quicksilver," "November," "The Poet Replies," "Dear Critic, Dear Abstraction," by Do Gentry, all original poems expressly written for this volume. Copyright © 2007 by Do Gentry.

"The Poet with Us: Nora May French," by Marvin R. Hiemstra, an original poem expressly written for this volume. Copyright © 2007 by Marvin R. Hiemstra.

ISBN-13: 978-0-9824296-6-2

Photograph of Nora May French by Arnold Genthe.
Cover design by Barbara Briggs Silbert.
Hippocampus Press logo designed by Anastasia Damianakos.

Published by Hippocampus Press
P.O. Box 641, New York, NY 10156

www.hippocampuspress.com

NORA MAY FRENCH
WAS BORN AT AURORA, NEW YORK,
APRIL THE TWENTY-SIXTH, 1881,
AND DIED AT CARMEL, CALIFORNIA,
NOVEMBER THE FOURTEENTH, 1907,
AGED TWENTY-SIX YEARS.

This edition of Nora May French's poems,
the only complete one since the original
of 1910, is dedicated to the memory of
the poet's only sister, Helen French Hunt,
1883–1973, dear and special friend,
as well as cherished patron and mentor,
to Donald Sidney-Fryer.

Acknowledgments

In redacting this augmented reprint volume of the *Poems* (1910) by Nora May French, the editors have incurred several salient debts of gratitude to various individuals and institutions. First, concerning information about the materials by and about Nora May French at the Bancroft Library, and their accessibility in divers collections (Judith Allen, Nora May French, James Marie Hopper, Henry Anderson Lafler, and George Sterling), we thank above everyone else Steven Black, Head of Acquisitions at the Bancroft. In putting together the Introduction to this volume, and no less the *Notes* and the *Notices*, Donald Sidney-Fryer as the senior editor has for the most part followed the lead of Judith Allen Gorog in her M.A. thesis "The Life and Writing of Nora May French" (1963), written for the English Department at Mills College, Oakland, California. Moreover, in much of the Introduction, the senior editor has based his text on that of Judith Allen Gorog's thesis, at times paralleling and following it quite closely.

All lovers of the extant poetry by Nora May French are indebted to Judith Allen Gorog for her pioneering monograph on Nora May French. Without her thesis, conducted with the assistance, encouragement, and unique personal resources of Nora May's only sister, Helen (Augusta) French Hunt, we would have very little information not only concerning the pre–San Francisco part of the poet's life and writing, but also concerning the sisters' general family background. In addition, we personally thank Judith Allen Gorog herself, presently residing in Lancaster, Pennsylvania, for reading most of our Introduction in its pre-final form.

A special debt of gratitude. In regard to the complicated love relationship between Henry Anderson Lafler and Nora May French (as well as, inferentially, between her and Captain Alan Hiley), whether conducted in letters or in person, covering the period from April 1905 through August 1907, we thank Dr. Joanne Lafler of Oakland for major or essential corrections, no less than her personal insights, deriving from her meticulously researched article about Henry Anderson Lafler, "The King of Telegraph Hill," published in the *Argonaut: Journal of the San Francisco Museum and Historical Society*, Summer 2004 (pp. 30–49). Dr. Lafler has based her scrupulous research on a detailed reconstruction and painstaking integration or interweaving—in the correct chronological sequence—of the extant Lafler–French correspondence (starting in April 1905 and ending sometime in 1906 or 1907), unfortunately and permanently divided between the Bancroft Library, University of California, Berkeley, in Northern California, and the Huntington Library, San Marino, in Southern California.

For permission to quote in full or in part from selected materials by and about Nora May French in their possession, we thank the Bancroft Library for the use of the unpublished poems "The Suicide" and "The Panther Woman" from the James Marie Hopper Papers, and "A Dream-Lover" from a letter to Lafler in the Henry Anderson Lafler Papers. Another unpublished poem, "Poppies," now part of the Nora May French Papers owned by the Bancroft Library, the senior editor copied when he had it in his possession along with other materials bequeathed to him by Helen French Hunt at her death on 9 April 1973. Likewise, for their assistance and warm cooperation, when we looked through materials by and about Nora May French for unpublished poems (we found none), especially in the correspondence between French and Lafler, and from George Sterling to Samuel Loveman, we thank the Huntington Library. We also thank the close friends and acquaintances who not only contributed the poems for the Tributes but also gave us the benefit of their perceptions and insights on divers aspects of Nora May French's life and personality. Most of all, we thank Helen French Hunt herself, in memoriam, for the unique inspiration that she furnished us unintentionally to undertake the task of seeing to the reprint of her sister's poems.

For permission to quote from correspondence between Sterling and Clark Ashton Smith, as well as from Smith's memoir "George Sterling: Poet and Friend" (as compiled and edited with other materials by David E. Schultz and S. T. Joshi in *The Shadow of the Unattained: The Letters of George Sterling and Clark Ashton Smith*, 2005), as relating to Nora May French and her poetry, we thank Derrick Hussey of Hippocampus Press, and William Dorman of CASiana Literary Enterprises, Sacramento, California.

For permission to reproduce the "Foreword," by Sara Bard Field, to the pamphlet *Poems by Nora May French*, issued in 1936, we thank the publisher, The Book Club of California, San Francisco.

Extraordinary thanks go to Do Gentry for formatting the manuscript for publication, the final stage of its preparation.

Contents

Acknowledgements 7
Nora May French: One Still, Small Voice Out of Time and Space 13
Sources 70
The Outer Gate: The Collected Poems of Nora May French 73
    The Outer Gate 75
    Rain 76
    Best-Loved 77
    The Rose 78
    Between Two Rains 79
    The Message 80
    By the Hospital 81
    "Oh, Dryad Thoughts" 82
    My Maid of Dreams 83
    Music in the Pavilion 84
    Rebuke 85
    In Camp 86
    The Nymph 87
    Vivisection 91
    The Stranger 92
    The Constant Ones 93
    Instinct 94
    The Lost Chimneys 95
    San Francisco, New Year's, 1907 96
    The Panther Woman 98
    The Poppy Field 99
    Poppies 100
    You 101
    Just a Dog 102
    Mirage 103
    Dusk 104
    THE SPANISH GIRL 105
    Part I 107
        I. The Vine 107
        II. The Chapel 108
        III. The Garden 109
        IV 110
        V 111
        VI 112
        VII 113

Part II 114
    I 114
    II 115
    III 116
    IV 117
    V 118
    VI 119
    VII 120
Part III 121
    I 121
    II 122
    III 123
    IV 124
    V 125
    VI 126
    VII 127
    VIII 128
The Garden of Dolores 129
Answered 130
Indifference 131
After-Knowledge 132
Be Silent, Love 133
Two Spendthrift Kings 134
Growth 135
Change 136
Wistaria 137
How Ends the Day? 138
My Nook 139
When Plaintively and Near the Cricket Sings 140
The Little Memories 141
Pass By 142
In Empty Courts 143
Down the Trail 144
"Bells from Over the Hills Sound Sweet" 146
In Town 148
Moods 149
A Misty Morning 150
Two Songs 151
Noon 152
Your Beautiful Passing 153
By Moonlight 154
A Dream-Love 155
One Day 156
The Mission Graves 157
Along the Track 158
A Place of Dreams 159

Think Not, O Lilias?	160
The Suicide	161
"To Rosy Buds . . . ."	162
Yesterday	163
The Mourner	164
Ave atque Vale	165
At the End	166

Notes **167**

Notices **173**
    General Note 175
    San Francisco *Bulletin*, Friday evening, 15 November 1907 175
    San Francisco *Call, Friday*, 15 November 1907 177
    San Francisco *Chronicle*, Friday, 15 November 1907. 180
    San Francisco *Chronicle*, Friday, 15 November 1907, notes 182
    San Francisco *Examiner*, Friday, November 15, 1907. 183
    Los Angeles *Times*, Friday, November 15, 1907 188
    Los Angeles *Times*, Sunday, November 17, 1907. 189
    Los Angeles *Times*, Monday, 18 November 1907. 190
    Town Talk, (Saturday,) 23 November 1907. 190
    Current Literature, June 1908. 192
    San Francisco *Call*, Sunday, June 12, 1910. 192
    The New Age, A Weekly Review of Politics, Literature and Art,
        Thursday, 14 July 1910. 193
    Current Literature, September 1910. 195
    Die Nieuwe Gids [The New Guidebook], November 1910. 196
    Poems by Nora May French, The California Literary Pamphlets,
        Number 2: 200
    Helen (Augusta) French Hunt (1883–1973): A little memoir
        (a friendship, 1968–1973) 204

Tributes **215**
    General Note 217
    Sources 217
    Untitled, *Henry Anderson Lafler* 219
    Sonnet, *Henry Anderson Lafler* 220
    Sonnet, *Henry Anderson Lafler* 221
    The Pearl, *Henry Anderson Lafler* 222
    Nora May French, *George Sterling* 228
    The Ashes in the Sea, *George Sterling* 229
    Nora May French, In Memoriam, *Louise Gebhard Cann* 231
    To Nora May French, *Clark Ashton Smith* 232
    "Thy Spirit Walks the Sea," *Donald Sidney-Fryer* 236
    [Nora May French], Dorothy Jesse Beagle 237
    For Nora May in Paradise, Mary Rudge 238
    Nora May, Alan Gullette 243
    For Nora May French, *Val Beatts* 243

Quicksilver, *Do Gentry* 244
November, *Do Gentry* 245
The Poet Replies, *Do Gentry* 246
Dear Critic, Dear Abstraction, *Do Gentry* 247
The Poet With Us: Nora May French, *Marvin R. Hiemstra* 248
Index of Titles 251
Index of First Lines 253

NORA MAY FRENCH:
ONE STILL, SMALL VOICE OUT OF
TIME AND SPACE

More than a hundred years have now passed since the death of the poet Nora May French in Carmel-by-the-Sea on the Monterey peninsula on 14 November 1907 at the early age of twenty-six, and not quite a hundred years have gone by since a group of close and influential friends published her one and only collection of surviving poems. During that passage of time the lore and legends about her have grown and prospered, even if her work per se has remained known largely to a small audience. Clearly she deserves an ampler readership, and perhaps this republication of her distinctive and individual poetry will help to achieve that consummation. Although born in upstate New York, and raised and educated mostly in the Los Angeles area of late Victorian times with its then unique mixture of Hispanic and Anglophone culture, Nora May has become identified with a certain group of poets and other writers located and flourishing primarily in Northern California during the approximate period 1890 to 1930.

This group has become identified as the California Romantics, which included Ambrose Bierce, George Sterling, Hermann Scheffauer, Nora May French, and Clark Ashton Smith among other figures. We could easily broaden membership in the group to include Jack London, if not in literary terms, assuredly then in personal ones. London and Sterling became friends in 1901 and socialized with each other as much as possible. Since the floruit of the California Romantics, some of its members—Bierce, Sterling, Smith, and certainly Nora May French as the outstanding woman poet of the group—have assumed by now the status of genuine Californian classics.

It might seem odd at first that the short period that Nora May spent in Northern California—a period of hardly more than a year and a few months from September 1906 to November 1907—should have thus identified her with this group; but however brief it may have turned out, that interim served to make more explicit her vocation, her true vocation, as poet, and her stature as literary personage. That interim also served to bring her to such maturity as she would manage to achieve before her early death. The California

Romantics resided over a fairly large expanse of territory, but it basically centered around the San Francisco Bay Area, including not only "the City," as it still is called, but just as much the communities located in and around that body of water. This area had outlying regions and connections: one extending on the north up to the Jack London fief at Glen Ellen in the Valley of the Moon; another reaching on the northeast much further, via the state capital at Sacramento, up to Auburn in the wide-spreading foothills of the Sierra Nevada mountains; and on the southwest yet another stretching down to the Monterey peninsula, perhaps even as far south as Big Sur.

The California of the late nineteenth and early twentieth centuries was quite a different place from what it is today. The state then would seem to us underpopulated or perhaps even unpopulated. Much of it still remained in the same natural condition that it had for centuries or even millennia before the arrival of the Europeans and then those Neo-Europeans known as the Americans, that is, of the United States. The natural beauty of California, startling in its variety and scope, spilled out abundantly everywhere, from the lush vegetation of its northern sector and its almost one thousand miles of coastline to the stark desert lands, beyond its long inland mountain ranges, all along its eastern and southern borders. Although the Los Angeles area, the nexus of Southern California, possessed already some real importance as an urban center with many smaller centers radiating from the hub in its commercial downtown, San Francisco still very much held its unique preeminence as the commercial and cultural focus of the North American west coast, as well as of this earlier and still comparatively pristine California.

This land was the California that Nora May French came to know well during her residence in the state from 1888 to 1907, and that made her and formed her into the thorough Californian that she became. However, by the time in 1888 that she emigrated with her family to Southern California from her birthplace in the Northeast, her first seven years in that former residence had already shaped her as a child, and moreover in a place of great natural beauty. Like her adopted California, that place commanded attention as a locus of striking native loveliness. Since Nora May could fit in one sense into the classification of nature poet, both her birthplace and California contributed to the kinship that she felt with nature, and in another sense to her becoming one of nature's many voices. Like many individuals, Nora May felt perhaps more comfortable ensconced in nature rather than with people, although she could certainly hold her own around them in any kind of social ambiance.

The poetry of Nora May French possesses its own kind of cosmic consciousness, aligning it well enough with the cosmic-astronomic-mindedness permeating the work of George Sterling and Clark Ashton Smith, which makes of their poetry a unique type of fantasy and science fiction in verse created long before such terms (in their current meaning) or such specialist magazines existed, but which does not quite make of her poetry the same thing. However, her work does partake of the general imaginative flair that exists in much popular art and literature before World War I. Those readers who know the general period of the California Romantics, the late nineteenth and early twentieth centuries, only through modern academic literature classes or textbooks have quite a surprise awaiting them if they should ever search through the magazines and newspapers of that period. Quite apart from its high technical quality, Nora May's poetry is not at all typical of such periodicals before the Great War. The considerable difference between most of the latter and her own work leaps out at the reader at once, and to Nora May's critical advantage. Although it evolved organically out of her life, her poetry is not autobiographical in the same sense that so much modern poetry characteristically has seemed since, say, the early 1920s. However, some knowledge of her life in depth and in detail appears essential to understanding her own poetry, the work of a woman who remains (in Kevin Starr's quintessential phrase) "hauntingly beautiful."

I

Nora May French was born on 26 April 1881 in the town of Aurora, on the eastern shore of Cayuga Lake in Cayuga County, situated in the western territory of upstate New York, amid the notable and picturesque region of the celebrated Finger Lakes, a rolling and hilly countryside of unusual natural beauty then as now, made up of open farmland alternating with deciduous woods and parklike areas. Not quite forty miles away to the northeast, Syracuse is the nearest city of any real size, and about the same distance to the north lies the vast ovaloid sheet of water called Lake Ontario, some 200 miles long east and west, some 50 miles wide north and south, and over 200 feet deep at its deepest—thus the first of the five great inland seas of fresh water known as the Great Lakes. Given her innate love of nature, this over-all geography alone would have made a profound impression on Nora May from infancy into early childhood.

An exceptional child, Nora May came of exceptional parents, who had in turn derived from exceptional families. The birth of her brothers had preceded that of Nora May as the first daughter in 1881, and then of the fourth and last child, the second daughter, Helen Augusta, in 1883, the sister who became Nora May's closest friend and confidante. Deriving from a family distinguished by at least one well-known lawyer and politician, his father Augustus C. French, Edward had planned to practice law in the town where the family of his wife Mary Wells resided, to wit, Aurora. A veteran of the Civil War (1861–65), Nora May's father had survived that conflict in good shape and had thus intended to emulate his father professionally, even if not politically: Augustus C. French had served as the Democratic governor of Illinois from 1846 to 1853.

The family of Nora May's mother seems no less distinguished. Henry Wells, Mary's brother, founded Wells, Fargo and Company, as well as the American Express Company, and then went on in Aurora to found and build Wells Seminary for Young Ladies in 1868, an institution that survives today as Wells College for Women. Both Henry and Mary claimed as father a Presbyterian clergyman, and Henry had begun as a mere express messenger, but in the space of a mere few years he owned not only the two express companies but several banks as well. By the time of his death, Henry had become a man of great wealth and great power. Following his death, the Wells family continued to dominate not just Wells College, but the entire town of Aurora.

Somehow the Wells family had persuaded Nora May's father to give up the practice of law to become a professor and college registrar at Wells, where he worked for sixteen years, apparently the span of time covering 1873–74 to 1887–88, and where he taught Latin, Latin literature, mathematics, and chemistry, betokening a Renaissance man or at least an individual with a very well-rounded education and capabilities. The evidence indicates that he functioned effectively as both professor and administrator, no less than as a loving family man.

Speaking for both Nora and herself, Helen French Hunt recalls as her earliest memories the quiet but full, and very good, life that the family enjoyed in and around Aurora. As literate parents from time immemorial have done, they read aloud to their children, shared with them their love of music, and took extended promenades with them in the rolling countryside around Aurora with its hills, deciduous woods, and little streams flowing into the beautiful good-sized lake. The entire family loved these leisurely walks, reveling in the natural beauty surrounding them on all sides. The children especially loved the live music in the evening, after they went to bed, while mother or father played the piano, and both would sing, leaving the door to the nursery open in response to the children's entreaties to hear these joyful sounds. Strengthening this love of music, the French family for several years had as house guest a German professor who served as the head of the music department at Wells, so that all during his sojourn with them this music-making, augmented by the professional musician in their midst, became a regular feature of many evenings.

Following the example of their parents, the children enjoyed good books, as well as reading to themselves and out loud. In particular Nora loved books and learned to read at the age of four. The parents maintained a very large library that featured a wide range of literature in prose and poetry. From this feast of exceptional treasures Nora loved above all the *Wonder Books* by Nathaniel Hawthorne, Graeco-Roman mythology (probably as purveyed from Bulfinch's *The Age of Fable*), the standard fairy tales, and quite a sampling of classic nonsense verse. The Victorian age had already provided many superb examples of such verse appropriate for children and families, above all as written by such master nonsense poets as Edward Lear, Lewis Carroll, and W. S. Gilbert, of Gilbert and Sullivan fame. This last love of Nora's would lead in later life to her very own well-turned humorous poems, most of which she and her family suppressed as not worthy of preservation in company with her serious poetry.

When Nora was seven and Helen five, this halcyonic family existence in Aurora came to an end. The family would soon leave upstate New York with its four preordained seasons, including the usual severe winter with ice and snow, for another, much milder climate in the far west of the United States, a land essentially with only two seasons, the hot and arid, and the cool and rainy—California. Their new home could not help but contrast with the northeastern part of the country. All through the 1880s, as a result of the great eruption of Krakatoa between Java and Sumatra in 1883, the winters in the northern latitudes all over the world were of unusual severity. Increasingly unhappy with teaching at Wells Seminary (which, he felt, did not put his education and interests to their best use), and chafing under the domination of his in-laws in so much of his personal, not to mention professional, existence, Edward French wanted freedom and a new life. Not far from the eastern edge of the great western ocean, he would find them on a small fruit ranch in a locale now known as Chevy Chase, in California, not far from southern Glendale. Edward and Mary French and their four children now moved to the Los Angeles area sometime during 1888.

"California fever" had taken possession of much of the rest of the country, but this second such excitement had as its goal the land in Southern California, unlike the first California fever that had the gold of Northern California as its object. The completion of the Santa Fe and Southern Pacific railroad lines in 1886–87 made a mass emigration from back east possible, and the price war deriving from the competition between the two railroad companies greatly reduced the fare to almost nothing. Civic boosters and enterprising realtors in Los Angeles took advantage of the price war by distributing thousands of advertising flyers throughout the nation, inducing people to purchase property and live in California, the land of (almost) eternal sunshine. During the later 1880s and early 1890s thousands of people entrained for the adventure of a new life, the realization of a new dream, in Southern California, where they purchased land to start life on a small brand-new fruit ranch. Almost everyone already in Southern California succumbed to the land-boom fever and speculated in the real-estate market. Whole families now flocked to the Los Angeles basin, bordered on the north and east by mountains that protected the region from much or most of the cold of the continental winters.

These newcomers included many professionals—doctors, teachers, farmers, lawyers, and businessmen of all types—but very few lasted long in their ranching venture. The French family lasted longer than most and held their little ranch for five years, until 1893. Evidently a ranch house with outbuildings either existed already or the parents had them especially constructed, which they could have afforded to do. Although they never made the ranch financially successful, the family managed to re-establish a mode of life somewhat like their old one in Aurora, but in an exotically different ambiance, with three hills, acres of sagebrush, and wild flowers as well as other plant life unlike those in the region of the Finger Lakes.

Edward French, who knew botany among other sciences, took the family on long promenades every week in these exciting new surroundings, identifying the new plants and animals. They thus came to know the new flora and fauna rather well, especially Nora May, who soaked up new impressions and would reproduce them in her later poetry, mingling them at times with impressions from elsewhere. Nature, its abundant beauty and ever-renewing variety, served as her great escape, her consolation, her special refuge, and her inspiration. Her early assimilation of nature whether in New York or in California, and the contrast between the two chief environments in which she grew up, set its indelible mark on her throughout her brief span of existence. As a poet Nora May French truly became "The Girl Who Made Friends with Nature."

Once again the family read aloud to each other, from the books that they had brought with them, especially the father: the Greek and Roman classics in the original language or in translation, the plays of Shakespeare, the British poets and novelists, Mark Twain and other Americans of that time, authors well suited to function as entertainment for the entire family. Once again the family played backgammon, cribbage, as well as word games, increasing the children's literacy. Once again music established its ancient and enduring claims, enchantments, and spiritual consolations. Both parents played piano, both parents could sing well, but the mother vocalized in an accomplished manner, and in addition the father played violin and flute. The girls learned to play the piano somewhat, but seemed most content to serve as a grateful audience. Helen retained her love of classical music to the end of her life, and Nora's innate musicality manifests itself in the individualized music of her poetry.

Although all the children seemed better than average students, Nora showed herself in particular an ardent learner, able to memorize easily and intelligently, and early on demonstrated remarkable creative ability. She started writing prose and poetry in her early adolescence, around the age of twelve. When in the mood for writing, she would vanish outdoors, into some out-of-the-way nook, and would rarely come back until she had finished whatever she was creating. Furthermore, besides her literary talent, she had already demonstrated a real talent for art through her inveterate sketching. Pleased and surprised by the creative skills Nora displayed, by their depth and clarity, the parents praised and encouraged them, and so with their warm support Nora proceeded on her way. Edward French in particular maintained his belief in his daughter's talent for literature and encouraged her up to her death.

We are emphasizing Nora's early years and education, going into considerable detail, because her experiences, her early and sustained contact with nature, formed her not just as a person but above all as the poet that she was becoming. Her education continued apace. At thirteen she commenced the study of Latin and Greek. Even though she did well enough, she never became the classical scholar that her father was. Sister Helen did better, but this branch of study the girls used mostly to give outlandish names to the pet cats that they liked to have around them! Nevertheless, the study of Latin and Greek, not to mention English, helped give both girls their easy command of rhetoric. Nora has evidenced this in her poetry and Helen in the compact and incisive letters she wrote to her close friends and relatives. Nora's apparent hypersensitivity found a balance in a pronounced sense of fun and humor, no less than in her love of nature and the countryside near Glendale. She wrote much comic verse, but only a few specimens exist. Otherwise this kind of verse might have served to balance out the rather pensive cast of her extant poems. According to sister Helen some of the humorous poems attained the rank of genuine comic gems; e.g., "The Ode on Aunt E.'s Bloomer Bathing Costume."

The family's life on the little fruit ranch continued in this quiet, pleasant manner when disaster struck. One of the worst economic depressions in American history spread all across the nation, following the land boom of the late 1880s and early 1890s, and it hit hardest in Southern California, ruining many farmers and their families. The situation was dire for a great many people, but for the French family it turned out worse. First of all, a catastrophic fire destroyed the ranch house and its contents. The family lost everything, including the father's extensive library and the mother's heirlooms. Later they lost the ranch itself through mortgage foreclosure. The father could no longer keep on ranching, and the family moved to Glendale. Edward obtained a position teaching in the Los Angeles public schools, where he taught for six years. Despite these difficulties the family survived, and life continued.

Through years of dislocation and relocation, Nora kept at her writing, which served as a kind of mental or emotional release for her, and which she did not always wish to share with others. The family respected this reticence, encouraged her, but did not interfere. In a series of interviews conducted by Judith Allen in February 1963, Helen described Nora's method of creation, especially her poetry, and cited one typical occasion. "Nora would be setting the table for dinner. As her concentration centered on the poetry, she would forget about the table, and still carrying the silverware, would walk dreamily around the table as she completed the verse, but not the setting."

Although her method of composition changed somewhat in later years, essentially it remained the same. Since she usually worked with metre and rime in her poems, Nora May generally carried the piece in her head while creating it, a method much easier to do than with a poem in free verse, or in free form, all of which usually demands redaction on paper at a desk. That last phase Nora reached only following the poem's completion in her mental workshop, although she would continue to modify and improve it, once she secured it on paper. This is the method used by many poets past or present, at least when working on a relatively short poem. Nora generally redacted the completed poem alone by herself out of doors or in some quiet nook indoors.

While well educated thanks to their parents, especially their professor father, the children had trouble staying in school because of the family's acute financial crisis. Nora May never finished her formal education, but the other children may have. In 1896 Nora, then fifteen, entered and dropped out of school twice, first in high school, next at Occidental Normal School (later Occidental College). In 1897 she entered and left Los Angeles Normal School (later UCLA). The family simply could not afford to put her through school. So she worked for several months at some job, then decided to enter art school to exploit her exceptional artistic talent for drawing, and eventually to make her career that of illustrator. In the autumn of 1898 Nora entered MacLeod Art School in Los Angeles, where she worked for tuition, room, and board. Her father came to take her out of school for an impromptu holiday during February 1899 so they could visit at his home Charles Lummis, pioneering editor of the progressive monthly magazine *Out West*, and an indefatigable booster as well as cultural leader of Southern California. But he was not at home that day. Lummis eventually published a dozen of Nora May's earliest poems, which fit nicely with the editor's California-themed preferences for poetry cast in traditional forms.

Sister Helen and other friends from around the fin-de-siècle remember Nora at eighteen as a beautiful young woman of great charm and pointed wit, but not unkind, albeit modest and accepting of both triumphs and reverses without making a fuss, including the problems faced by her parents in particular. Somehow Edward lost his teaching position, and without complaint or demur, given the family's financial crisis, Nora left art school. She found a job in a carved-leather factory, where her skill at drawing proved essential for the pictorial representations realized on leather products. She and the family did all that they could to cheer up Edward, who had become severely depressed. During some weekend sojourn to Long Beach on the then interurban electric trains, the family took a needed holiday from their troubles. An Italian-American orchestra gave free concerts in the Park Pavilion in that city, and the family attended one of their concerts, evidently sitting close to the orchestra. Nora forthwith began sketching the musicians at their labor, which delighted and charmed them. Nora's blond beauty would certainly have caught their attention in any event. They returned the compliment by performing with even greater sentiment, and out of this experience emerged the touching and vivid poem "Music in the Pavilion," which captures a transient but poignant moment at a Sunday concert.

Despite the reverses endured by the family or by Nora herself, she remained resolutely cheerful. A good piece of luck now befell the young artist and poet. Some relatives on the East Coast offered her a wonderful opportunity. A wealthy uncle in New York City wrote to his brother Edward French, asking if Nora would like to study art there while living with the uncle's family. She would thus not need to worry about tuition, room, or board. Such a prospect brought the entire family great joy, and the parents and Nora herself accepted the offer. Presumably the family's finances had improved to the point where they could dispense with the income that Nora had been bringing into the household. She traveled back to her native state in the autumn of 1899 to the great city that she had evidently never visited before. Settling in at her uncle's house, she began her first year of study, 1899–1900. She first attended the New York Students League, but later entered the Chase School of Design for the more practical training offered there in terms of future employment. Once she had completed her studies, Nora would have to support herself, of course.

After her difficulties attending school in Los Angeles, and after the need for her to work at the leather factory, the school year back east emerged as the single happiest period in her life. Nora May could now concentrate on her art and studies, she had no financial worries, and she enjoyed the great metropolis thoroughly. Meanwhile she continued her writing, both poems and articles, some of them already published in the *Los Angeles Times Magazine* (on Sunday), starting in the spring of 1894. Her father constantly urged her to keep at her writing. He himself was writing both stories and articles but encountered little success at selling them. However, after only one year of study, Nora returned home to Glendale, the wonderful interlude in Gotham had ended. With further study there impossible, she returned to designing in the leather factory. The management had now gained back an even more valuable employee.

What had gone wrong back east? Problems of an unexpected kind had come about in the uncle's household, caused inadvertently by Nora's presence. As confidentially told to the present writer by Helen French Hunt herself, the uncle's children included a very handsome cousin, a youth about Nora's age. The two beautiful young people had fallen deeply in love, but apparently had not consummated their love physically—not surprisingly, given the customs and morals of late Victorian times. It was not just their mutual youth and beauty that had attracted them to each other, but they shared much else in common as two young sensitive people. Nora May could not, would not, have fallen in love if she could not have communed with her cousin on a very deep level. However, once their love was discovered, to prevent any problems from arising in the future, Nora's uncle decided that she should return to Los Angeles as soon as possible relative to the school year. Thus ended the happiest period in her life, which also concluded with what emerged as a wrenching emotional disappointment for Nora. We can imagine the welter of conflicting emotions that she suffered on her return trip by train to Southern California.

Rising above these personal and professional disappointments as best she could, the poet-artist continued working at the leather factory until sometime in the spring of 1906. During these half-dozen years or so, 1900–1906, a period of steady employment as well as poetic productivity, Nora continued writing, and she also read widely, especially in poetry. It is of significance to note that, in addition to the acknowledged classics—Coleridge, Wordsworth, Keats, Shelley, Tennyson, Longfellow together with others—she kept abreast of the works of contemporary or modern poets: Walt Whitman, Edward FitzGerald, Robert Browning, Rudyard Kipling, John Masefield, A. E. Housman, and William Butler Yeats. As pointed out by George Sterling, two poets in particular exercised the greatest influence on Nora's own poems: Tennyson and Housman, the latter both a poet and a classical scholar. Indeed, between the young woman's works and those in the famous collection by Housman, *A Shropshire Lad*, with its bittersweet mood or tone, we can perceive at times a marked resemblance in both form and content. It goes without saying that Nora knew by instinct how to rise above mere imitation in order to utilize any and all influences as a vehicle for her own personal feelings and purposes.

Sometime during this period Nora worked as an assistant editor for a so-called little magazine, but it gave up the ghost after a few months. Meanwhile Lummis continued to publish her poems in *Out West* until 1905. Altogether he featured twelve of her earliest poems, and Nora's posthumous editors and publishers included them all in the volume of 1910 except "Answered." This poem anticipates not only the fate meted out to Dolores in "The Spanish Girl," Nora's later tour de force—that of a young maiden cut down in the flowering of her youth and beauty—but also Nora's own tragic and early death. Although she got along well evidently with everyone and could hold her own socially, she absolutely needed her periods of withdrawal, when she could commune with herself, could regain her emotional balance, but above all else could create her poetry, at once her solace and a form of prayer for her, as it were.

Nora's lively charm and exceptional beauty captured much attention, and many men, it seems, more often young than otherwise, paid court to her. She herself, since her twelfth year, had often fallen in and out of love, albeit never to the point of coition. At that period in history, and as in many cultures today, women usually saved consummation for marriage, and Nora had not yet seriously considered marriage. The affair with her handsome cousin in New York City had evolved into Nora's first serious love, and now her second affair materialized. Like her cousin, this newcomer happened to be an exceptional individual: Captain Alan Hiley, handsome, intelligent, cultivated, a dashing British soldier-of-fortune complete with black moustache. Hiley had come down to Los Angeles on some business or other from the lumber ranch that he owned and ran in the Santa Cruz Mountains just north of the Monterey peninsula and Monterey Bay. Somehow poet-artist and timber-rancher moved into each other's orbit. Alan met Nora and fell in love with her, and soon in turn she fell in love with him. With this man, as with her cousin, a rare thing happened: Nora could conduct a real conversation in depth, such as she could not achieve with most men. Unfortunately, Captain Hiley was already married, but he hoped soon to be divorced. However, his wife seemed to be going out of her way to make their ultimate separation as awkward and protracted as possible.

As wonderful as it was to be in love with a man who conformed to her own preferred ideal in all respects, Nora now underwent a very difficult period of considerable anguish and unhappiness, as often happens when the emotional stakes turn out so high. Marriage between Alan and Nora seemed impossible. Nora's common sense combined with social pressures from friends and family alike, and she withdrew from him, something that must have proven extremely hard to do. However, she did derive one great good thing out of this affair, her second serious love: during this emotionally tumultuous period she created, but did not perfect, the major portion of her introspective masterpiece "The Spanish Girl" (evidently the first two of the three parts). Like any good suitor worth his salt, although he acquiesced as graciously as possible, Captain Hiley did not give up hope of eventually winning Nora as his wife, and would still visit Los Angeles on occasion, to try and make Nora change her mind.

Nora May had had the good fortune, or misfortune, to be raised by parents between whom an unusually fine relationship existed, one that included a complete sharing on all levels—physical, intellectual, spiritual—with a full conversational exchange. This ideal type of union had permanently marked Nora May, and this was the type for which she hungered, and apparently could not find with most of her suitors, generally dependable and decent young chaps. Nora would become engaged to some apt young man, only to break the engagement later on. She did not want a conventional union, but (in old-fashioned parlance) a soulmate. She rarely found such a partner. Whether in person or in correspondence (confirmed by sister Helen), she raved ferociously against the conventional ideal that marriage in and of itself should form the terminal objective of a woman's life or her particular ambitions without the complete sharing on which she insisted. In a sense the ideal union such as her parents had afforded their children ultimately became the obstruction, the reef, upon which the vessel that was her life would crash and in whose wake she would perish.

Sometime evidently during the winter of 1904–05, the writer Mary Austin made one of her occasional visits to San Francisco. She had just published one of her best books, *The Land of Little Rain* (1903), a collection of penetrating essays on southeastern California. An adopted Californian like Nora May, as well as a pronounced mystic, Austin also wrote on occasion for *Out West* and had evolved an enthusiastic admiration for Nora May's poems. Although some found Austin's general enthusiasm rather fatiguing, most of them respected her literary judgment. While in the City, she sang continuously in praise of Nora as a poet, and the lovers of fine literature there sat up and took notice, seeking out the young woman's poetry. Austin must have read some of the poems aloud and otherwise passed them around.

One person especially became quite impressed, the man of letters Henry Anderson Lafler, and his own enthusiasm counted for something, in his position as literary editor for the *Argonaut*, as well as editor of his own later publication, the *Blue Mule*, a short story magazine. Born on 6 February 1878 at Gaines, a farming town in the extreme northwest corner of western New York State, and about a hundred miles west-northwest of that Aurora where Nora May had herself come into this world, Lafler passed his childhood and adolescence in the same small town that had witnessed his birth. In the later 1890s he went west to Nebraska, attending for two years the University of Nebraska at Lincoln. Around 1900 he went yet further west to San Francisco, where he proceeded to establish himself in magazine writing and editing, also becoming part of the Bohemian community there. Lafler wrote to Nora May, asking to publish her poems. She consented, and an exchange of letters and poems began between them in the spring of 1905. This exchange would not end until she moved to San Francisco during the summer of 1906, although she and Lafler may have still exchanged an occasional note in 1907 when both were living in Northern California.

The French family, sometime around 1901 or a little later, had moved to Los Angeles. The two brothers had already moved out of the household to pursue their own lives and careers by 1905. The two sisters were now caring for their mother during a painful and protracted illness. Mary Wells French died in July 1905. The daughters now moved together into an apartment and worked to pay the family's bills. Almost blind from cataracts, Edward French went to the Old Soldiers' Home (later the Veterans Administration) in Westwood near Santa Monica with its hospital, dormitories, chapel, and administration buildings. There he had an operation to restore his eyesight. As a Civil War veteran, Edward could claim a legitimate right to any and all medical services. With eyesight restored well enough, he decided to stay on at the installation as a clerk in the records office, but on the weekends he would return to Los Angeles (now downtown L.A.) to visit with his daughters at their shared apartment. Otherwise the family had no regular home and never came together again in a shared household.

Necessity dictated, of course, that both sisters work, and they found a measure of stability in their love and friendship for each other. The departure of their brothers out of the old household, the mother's death, the father's residence in Westwood—all this resulted in the young women growing very close to each other. At that period in American history, most jobs demanded that employees work six days a week, almost the same as when most people worked as subsistence farmers with one day of rest, the Sabbath or seventh day of the week. In addition to her regular job six days a week as designer-artist, Nora May wrote as often as possible—poetry, articles, letters, whatever—as time and energy allowed. At twenty-four years of age, she generally had enough energy, but sister Helen often worried about her occasional want of vitality.

The burgeoning relationship with Lafler acting as her poetic mentor gave Nora a special escape-valve and was quite a welcome intellectual and emotional outlet. It also became quite important to Lafler, who was falling in love with her. Their correspondence soon grew from a trickle into a flood between the spring of 1905 and the fall of 1906. Many of their letters have disappeared, except for the small but sizable amount preserved at the Bancroft and Huntington libraries. The correspondence that survives (especially that of August 1905, although some is undated) lets us know just how Nora's poems grew directly out of her life. Gathered together and edited, the surviving letters might make a worthwhile volume of intimate correspondence.

As Nora reported in her letters, neither she nor Helen lacked for suitors in the form of young men; but these decent and well-intentioned youths, while offering the financial security that the sisters' parents had enjoyed only intermittently, lacked everything else that the sisters wanted to share with their partners—a love of literature, music, and art along with the long outdoor walks that they and their parents had enjoyed, and that the girls living together still enjoyed. During this interim Nora continued creating the remarkable and usually nature-oriented poems that went into her posthumous collection. The new poems that she shared with her new mentor include these about which their letters inform us: "Two Spendthrift Kings," "The Message," "Be Silent, Love," "Remembered Faces," "Ave atque Vale," "In Camp," and "The Spanish Girl," Part III. "Remembered Faces" apparently does not survive.

In her letter of 22 August 1905, Nora let it be known that she preferred the name of Phyllis, a nickname going back into her childhood, or so she claimed (something not necessarily confirmed by her sister). But later in Northern California, when people addressed her as Phyllis in Helen's presence, the older sister explained to her nonplussed sibling that they called her Phyllis because they disliked the name of Nora. This all may seem rather capricious or disingenuous on Nora's part until we recall that she had a great sense of humor. These names, interestingly, have curious historical resonances. Nora or Norah derives from such Latinate appellations as Honora, Leonora, Eleanor; and Phyllis derives from the Greek word for a green bough, not at all inappropriate for someone writing nature-oriented poems!

For his part, aside from acting as her poetic mentor in letters, Lafler later in person would describe at length San Francisco and Carmel along with the persons and places that he wanted Nora to see whenever she could come up north, to visit or even to live there. Of course, he was hoping that she would remain and forsake Southern California. In particular he told her of the solid and substantial Montgomery Building in downtown San Francisco, otherwise known as the Monkey Block, replaced today by the Transamerica Building (built in 1980). The original building dated back to 1852 and had survived fires and earthquakes. Lafler also told her about Coppa's, the restaurant located on the ground floor of the Monkey Block, owned and operated by Giuseppi Coppa, a Turinese chef and bon vivant. Because he had helped feed many a poor artist or writer, "Pop" Coppa had become a cultural hero to the Bohemians then living in the City.

Out of gratitude and with Coppa's permission, of course, a variety of well-known writers and artists had covered the three walls above the dado in the main dining chamber (the fourth wall had windows looking out into the street) with all manner of strange and whimsical creatures and sayings, such as were deemed suitable to the true spirit of Bohemia, and as were deployed in scrolls, plaques, and other decorative caprices. The curious murals soon made Coppa's eatery famous or infamous from coast to coast, and thanks to Lafler, even Nora had a quotation from one of her letters displayed on high: "I fancy that all sensible people will ultimately be damned." This remark became quoted and repeated all over town, or so Lafler reported back to the sisters in Los Angeles: Nora had gained renown even before she headed north.

Taking a short holiday from the *Argonaut*, Lafler at last journeyed south to meet Nora in person, evidently in January 1906. They had exchanged photos of each other, but both mutually feared that a meeting in person might ruin the friendship. Just the opposite happened. They fell in love and physically consummated their attraction. Lafler was a handsome, well-built, and charismatic man. Nora had once more plunged into the same kind of situation that she had with Captain Hiley. Estranged from his wife, Lafler had not yet filed for divorce. No real future seemed possible for the union of Lafler and Nora May. He hied himself back to the City, and they began their correspondence again. Despite this latest turn of events, Alan Hiley continued to visit Los Angeles and to hope that he might yet win Nora's hand. Not just because of his rivalry, the good captain had no great love for Lafler, a distaste that sister Helen shared as time went on, a distaste perhaps not unmerited in light of what would happen.

Under the inspiration of Lafler's guidance and encouragement, Nora continued her poetic productivity. She had a bad habit of scribbling some poems rapidly, and then, dissatisfied with them, she would throw them away. Lafler suggested that, whenever she had such doubts about their worth, she should send the poems to him, and he would give counsel accordingly. Lafler thus managed to preserve many poems that otherwise would have disappeared, as for example "Be Silent, Love," rewritten in February 1906. Some have irretrievably vanished, it would seem, such as "Remembered Faces." Another, "Ave atque Vale," (that is, "Hail and Farewell"), Nora wrote two years before she died, that is, around November of 1905. This poem has a curious genesis.

Lafler on occasion used this phrase in his letters, and the poet-artist adapted the phrase and concept for the title and content of her own poem. However, she would have known the standard phrase from the time when she and Helen had studied Latin and Greek with their father. A few days before her death, Nora mailed the poem to the magazine *Sunset*, and the press presumed that it represented her very last or farewell poem, which it did not. Sometime during the winter of 1905–06 Nora was finishing "The Spanish Girl," her single most ambitious poem or interrelated series of poems. This was Part III, the conclusion of the work. Whatever else we may think of Lafler in a personal way, all admirers of Nora May French's poems bear him a large debt of gratitude for encouraging her to create and polish all the poems that she redacted under his mentorship.

Above and beyond this tutelage, Lafler in his letters encouraged "Phyllis" over and over again to move north and to live in the City. There she could find the companionship of like-minded people, artists and writers of all kinds, that she could not find in the provincial Los Angeles of that period, a companionship that might inspire and stimulate her. Also, working out of San Francisco through Lafler and his friends, she would have far greater access to publishers, whether on the West or East Coast, than if she stayed in Southern California, then deemed a very limited locale by comparison.

Meanwhile, having heard of the gifted and lovely sisters through Lafler, the artist and mystic Bruce Porter went south to meet them in person. General artist, landscape designer, muralist, book designer, and maker of stained-glass windows, Porter had not only made an excellent reputation for himself but had even earned his living for some length of time through his various arts and crafts. He sojourned in Los Angeles for several months, probably late winter and early spring of 1906. Although he presented himself as a suitor to both young ladies, they did not respond to his courting seriously, but simply became his friends. They did like him and his company quite a bit. Handsome, animated, imaginative, and reasonably successful, Porter might have made a good husband for either sister. He shared some of their interests and often accompanied them on their long promenades, no less than on their day trips on weekends.

Porter had become their "pet," and they called him "Bru." He still was living in Los Angeles and paying them court when "Phyllis" made a momentous decision, the most important in her life now seen in retrospect. She would move to San Francisco to try and make a career for herself there as a writer. But something happened in the Bay Area to postpone her plans. On 18 April 1906 a very strong earthquake without precedent in living memory struck San Francisco, succeeded at once by a fire that burned for three days, unchecked except by dynamiting along the edges of the conflagration.

Lasting only a minute or less, the earthquake itself, the most destructive in American history, had convulsed the City at 5:12 A.M. It ruptured the gas lines and started innumerable fires, which soon united into one enormous blaze. The flames reached as high as twenty stories. The temperature of the conflagration exceeded 2,000 degrees Fahrenheit, hot enough to melt steel. The earthquake had also ruptured the water lines, and the City had no water to fight the fires. When the fires finally burned out, the conflagration left an estimated 3,000 people dead, 28,000 buildings destroyed, 500 city blocks making up a total of five square miles incinerated, and out of a population of not quite half a million, some 250,000 homeless. The fire had consumed much but not all of the City, largely the area bounded on the west by Van Ness Avenue and on the south by somewhere below Market or Mission Streets. Obviously Nora May could do little either for herself or for San Francisco in such a situation. Therefore she decided to wait out the next five months in Southern California and to keep on working six days a week at her regular job, saving as much money as possible for the big move north.

Later that same spring of 1906 Nora gave notice at the leather factory, and the two sisters moved to a secluded camp in Santa Anita Canyon to reside there during the summer. There they would live quietly until September, as it turned out. Helen often worried about Nora's health, especially her lack of vitality, and felt that perhaps just plain rest, together with the mountain air and general ambiance, would restore her sister's health. The simple camp life agreed with both of them, especially Nora. Helen's plan worked, Nora's health improved. They had a very good time together, talking, walking, sketching, resting. The lack of any real stress helped both of them enormously. Nora recorded her impressions in the poem "In Camp," which commemorated that halcyonic summer in such a remote spot. The sisters debated Nora's future. Helen did not want her to go north—was this a premonition?—and preferred that Nora remain and write in Southern California. Nora did not agree, and the sisters had a rare quarrel. That September, while Helen retreated to the apartment in Los Angeles, her dear but determined sister took the train to Northern California, where at long last she would start a new life for herself in San Francisco while it continued to rebuild itself.

II

In late summer or early autumn, Nora Nay French arrived in San Francisco. Lafler might very well have met her at the train station somewhat south of the main or downtown area. At that period one reached San Francisco by the ferry-boat system that plied throughout the Bay Area, or by the railroad that came north up through the San Francisco peninsula from San Jose through San Mateo County just to the south of the City. The beautiful young poet now stood at the very threshold of her new life, her great adventure, so long anticipated and so long delayed. Nora May's great charm and blond beauty, coupled with her acknowledged poetic talent, would have struck everyone who had not already met her.

Chief among all those artists preeminent in the Bay Area at that time who would have long since sat up and taken notice of Nora May's poems when Mary Austin touted them in 1903—and far more significant than Lafler whether as Nora's mentor or as literary editor of the *Argonaut*—stood George Sterling, strikingly handsome, slender but well-built, charismatic, then in his later thirties, and recognized in the City and elsewhere as a great poet. The group that he now headed included as well, whether strictly Bohemian or not, such survivors of California's earliest artistic and literary flowering as Ambrose Bierce (now living on the east coast) and, over in Oakland, the poet and former librarian Ina Donna Coolbrith, the doyenne and inspiratrix of poets and other artists.

When in 1890 he had come to California, Sterling began working in the office of the real-estate magnate Frank C. Havens, his wealthy uncle in Oakland, with the goal of pursuing a business career, but he was now shifting over into his true vocation, that of poet and man of letters. Under the tutelage of Ambrose Bierce (born in 1842), California's Great Cham of Letters— satiric writer, storyteller, critic, and poetic mentor—Sterling had produced his first mature poetry during the late 1890s and early 1900s. He had gathered these first fruits into his first collection, *The Testimony of the Suns* (published first in 1903 by W. E. Wood, and then in 1904 and 1907 by A. M. Robertson, who became Sterling's regular publisher). The volume helped to establish Sterling as the leading poet of the West Coast, and as the unofficial poet laureate of San Francisco and Carmel. From 1890 to 1905 he worked for his wealthy uncle. He had married Carolyn (or Carrie) Rand in February 1896, living in Oakland not far from Jack London, whom Sterling first met in 1901, after which they had become the closest of friends.

Sterling had completed in January 1904 what would become his most celebrated long poem "A Wine of Wizardry," although it was not yet published. Ranked as highly by some experts as Coleridge's masterpiece of pure poetry, "Kubla Khan," "A Wine of Wizardry" had already circulated in typed manuscript among various men of letters in Northern California. First, it had won the highest praise of Bierce himself, then residing at the Army and Navy Club in Washington, D.C., who had advised Sterling on this poem but lightly, who became at once its greatest champion, and who would eventually secure its first publication in a national magazine in 1907. Two of its most imaginative lines—"The blue-eyed vampire, sated at her feast, / Smiles bloodily against the leprous moon"—had already gained their greatest notoriety on one of the walls of Coppa's Italian restaurant in the Monkey Block, when some artist had emblazoned them in an appropriate scroll.

The Havens had apparently reacted favorably to their nephew's new vocation—the aunt-by-marriage Lila Rand Havens was the sister of the poet's wife Carolyn—and by some pre-agreement George now received his reward, beyond his salary, for his extended service in his uncle's employ when the Havens gave him his "freedom money," as George dubbed it. With his wife, Sterling emigrated from Piedmont in Oakland down to Carmel, acquired some property, and built a shack that soon evolved into a bungalow. Later he built, alongside it, a tent-house that evolved into a cabin. He also kept a small tent. He had gone to Carmel to sequester himself so that he could concentrate on his poetry and other writing without distraction, a plan that did not quite work out through no fault of Sterling's. George and Carrie were always inviting friends down from the Bay Area.

Soon other artists and writers had followed Sterling down to the new Shangri-La, and after the earthquake and fire of 1906 the group increased to a considerable size, and many of them had erected shacks, tents, and cabins, wherein they proceeded to live, at least in the warmer weather. Even if not intentionally, Sterling had established Carmel as the artists' colony that it increasingly became with the passage of time. Thus as the real but inadvertent founder of Carmel, George moved back and forth, sometimes with his wife, sometimes not, between Carmel and the general Bay Area, sometimes staying with his relatives, sometimes not.

Into this fully formed Bohemian community centered both in Carmel and San Francisco, and headed by George Sterling, Nora May French now made her entrance. It is heartening to note just how cordially this community welcomed her into their midst. Lafler might have helped her find some appropriate lodging, unless she stayed with him, at least overnight. Some reliable details about Lafler and Nora May at this time have come to light in Joanne Lafler's cogent and meticulously researched article "The King of Telegraph Hill." Lafler was building the first of several bungalows on Telegraph Hill on a lot whose use he had obtained from Sterling's uncle Frank C. Havens, but Nora may not have lived there. She did find herself a rented room on Chestnut Street, and by January 1907 she had moved into a cottage on Lombard Street. Here she would live, and with her sister from March 1907, into August of the same year.

Lafler might very well have acted as Nora's first guide around the City, much of which had survived the earthquake and fire. Since the catastrophe San Francisco has grown to four times its original size, the latter primarily restricted to the northeastern fourth of San Francisco County, the metropolis itself occupying today the same terrain as the county, representing the northern end—some seventy square miles—of the San Francisco peninsula. The cleaning up and rebuilding of the destroyed part of the City had commenced at once and were actively going forward by the time of Nora's arrival. The major districts that had survived included the Marina (the much smaller area before the Exposition of 1915), Cow Hollow, Pacific Heights (essentially a continuation of the destroyed Nob Hill area), the enormous Fillmore, the elegant faubourg of the Haight-Ashbury, the spacious Mission district, and Diamond Heights among other regions. Although the fire destroyed some thirty city blocks in the northern or northwestern section, most of the original Mission district (the original Hispanic nucleus of the later City) had survived, especially the old and beloved Mission Dolores.

In the area almost totally destroyed, some special buildings had managed to survive, but only thanks to special circumstances: the grand fin-de-siècle U.S. Post Office at Mission and Seventh Streets, the stout and solid U.S. Mint at Mission and Third (opened in 1874), and a very small number of similar landmarks. Thus enough of the City had survived to give a sensitive newcomer like Nora May a real concept of what the metropolis looked like before the catastrophe. Nora May fell in love at once with San Francisco, as well as with the surrounding (and then underpopulated) Bay Area, including Berkeley, Oakland, and Sausalito. In this instant love she resembled many others before or since, fascinated by the area's manifold and shifting moods as furnished by fog or sunlight, and as affected by the enormous ridge of Twin Peaks running north and south through the middle of the City. Its compact and European atmosphere and layout must have also impressed the young poet, so different as it was from Los Angeles.

It was probably Lafler, acting as her eager cicerone, who presented the beautiful newcomer to all those people whom he had already described to Nora May. Sterling complimented her at once on her poetic talent. Living in the Piedmont section of Oakland, Jack and Charmian London invited her to dinner. The erudite and witty man of letters Porter Garnett, later a fine printer of national eminence, evidently made a sympathetic impression on Nora, because she would create a sonnet for his wedding in the spring of 1907. Blanche Partington, who maintained a kind of literary salon in her home, not only requested the new poet's presence at her evenings, but even offered to help her find periodical publication for her poems. A friend of the Londons and Sterlings, Blanche acted as a kind of patroness and inspiratrix to many writers and artists, and her generous help counted for something.

Through Lafler or the Sterlings, Ina Coolbrith in Oakland invited Nora to one of her gatherings: Ina's good opinion of Nora's poetry, no less than her immediate liking for her personally, was also of value. Through the same channels Nora met the painter Xavier ("Marty") Martinez and his youthful betrothed Elsie Whitaker, the journalists Will and Wallace Irwin, and the droll and erudite Gelett Burgess, author of the two famous quatrains about "The Purple Cow." In addition to all these fascinating artistic and literary people, Nora became surrounded by all kinds of admirers, all of them charming and cultivated. She had certainly arrived, and in more ways than one. Thus receiving total acceptance, Nora became one with them and participated in their debates, readings, and celebrations. Those who remember her from this period recall not only her great charm, her good-natured wit, but her striking blond beauty, her moodiness, and her strange "luminous eyes." Altogether, the period of her San Francisco residence presented quite a contrast to her former limited life in the City of the Angels.

According to Joanne Lafler, in her article "The King of Telegraph Hill," it was in August 1906, not long after her arrival in Northern California, that Nora went south to Carmel with Lafler, the first of many visits there before her death. It was on this occasion that Nora first met George and Carrie Sterling. Just as she had done with San Francisco, Nora now fell in love at once with the spectacularly beautiful countryside in and around Carmel, the valley, the river, the beaches, the woods, the headlands, and the then almost complete lack of development. Everything would still have seemed marvelously pristine and primordial. George liked Nora May at once, but initially

Carrie did not care for her; she perceived her as a freak with too much happening in her life. Later Carrie would correct this first impression and would come to have great affection for Nora.

Nora's relationship with Lafler had now reached a critical stage of development. Eight years after her death, in a letter dated 9 January 1916, to the fine lyrical poet and bibliophile Samuel Loveman, Sterling bore witness to the now complete love relationship between Lafler and Nora. George stated unequivocally: "She was his mistress from the time she left Los Angeles (to come to S.F.) till the day of her death [. . .]." (This letter is preserved with others from Sterling to Loveman in the Huntington Library, San Marino, California.) Actually, sometime after August 1907, Lafler and Nora seem to have parted, evidently for good. However, if anyone would have known about the state of the love affair between Lafler and Nora, George certainly would have, given his close friendship with Lafler.

This privileged information, which Lafler would not have shared with just anyone, would therefore give some kind of credence to the rumors making the rounds only much later that apparently Nora had one or more abortions before her death, and that the abortions, or their necessity, could only have come about because of her liaison with Lafler. According to Joanne Lafler, Nora had become pregnant during the winter of 1905–06 by her lover, and her sister Helen later recorded that Nora had had an illegal operation to terminate the pregnancy. This led to her entering the hospital that same winter, evidently to recover from the effects of the illicit abortion. Such operations would help to explain at least in part Nora's intermittent lassitude and lack of vitality, and her consequent depression. Even under the best of circumstances, abortions notoriously take a great deal out of a woman whether physically, emotionally, or spiritually.

Sometime that autumn of 1906, evidently late in the season, and extending on into the winter of 1906–07, Nora became seriously ill. She caught a bad cold that developed into pleural pneumonia, forcing her to remain for at least several weeks in some hospital in San Francisco, where she still managed to write both poems and letters to friends, giving news of herself and her sister in Los Angeles. She wanted Helen to live with her as soon as possible, but a serious illness, typhoid fever, had likewise forced her sister to spend at least several weeks at some hospital in Southern California. As it turned out, Helen could not come up north until March 1907, about a half-year after Nora's arrival there. While in the hospital, Nora wrote at least several poems. Lafler and Partington, who contributed to the magazine, urged Nora to begin submitting poems to *Sunset*. The unofficial publication of the Southern Pacific Railroad, this periodical at that time had an agenda like that of Charles Lummis for *Out West*, to boost California through fiction, articles, and poetry dealing with the Far West, and thus to encourage tourism and emigration from back east.

Two of the poems from Nora's hospital stay have survived. A humorous poem, "The Lost Chimneys," dealt with Santa's problems delivering toys that Christmas of 1906. She had conceived the poem in the same humorous mode as many native popular-style effusions of that time published in the City. She sold the poem to *Sunset*, one of the few humorous ones by Nora that have survived, and it appeared in the issue for December 1906. Also while in the hospital, Nora created another "seasonal" poem, also dealing with the earthquake's aftermath but in a serious and somber mode, "San Francisco, New Year's, 1907," wherein the poet seems to revel in nature's power to destroy, reminding us that forces exist much stronger than humankind, too often preoccupied with its trivial concerns and its petty lives, to the exclusion of everything else.

Ever considerate, Sterling came around Christmas to visit her in the hospital and gave her, as a thoughtful and appropriate gift, an edition of poems by Keats, in which he had written an inspiring dedication: "When you meet Keats in the poet's Elysium, may I be there to see." Certainly this captured George's high regard for Nora May's poems, and this generous admiration could only have encouraged her to continue her serious efforts on behalf of poetry among other avenues of expression. Sometime after New Year's Day, the hospital discharged her, and Nora resumed her customary life. Some friends may possibly have held a little celebration in honor of her discharge from the hospital and her having survived the serious illness that had confined her. She once more reapplied herself to her poems, reworking and recasting them, even if she continued on occasion to scribble certain verses that she then found unworthy and subsequently discarded. However, the encouragement and in a sense the sponsorship of Nora May and her poetry by Sterling were significant. Both Helen and Nora knew Sterling's own poetry in depth, not only his first volume, *The Testimony of the Suns*, but also "A Wine of Wizardry" when it was circulating in manuscript.

Whatever other problems Nora may have had, they did not stem either from her not taking herself seriously or from lack of appreciation from others. The winter of 1906–07 continued quietly, without any further crisis, and in March Helen arrived from Southern California to live once again with Nora.

They resided in a cottage on Lombard Street. Here they would live until late August 1907 and would re-create a life similar to that in Los Angeles, but in an exciting new metropolitan ambiance. First, however, they each got themselves a job, Nora going to work as a telephone operator in San Francisco. She would keep this job from early spring until late August, during which time an extended strike took place there throughout the summer of 1907. Since she did not join the strikers but chose to work as a "scab" during the entire strike, it is evident that neither Nora nor Helen could afford not to work, and that they needed both their salaries to live adequately in the City. They had neither friends nor family to support them if they did not work.

However, out of this experience would emerge the only known professional short story by Nora May French, "The Diary of a Telephone Girl," a worthwhile effort in every way. She sold it to the *Saturday Evening Post*, and it appeared in the issue for 19 October 1907. (According to her sister Helen, Nora had contributed both stories and prose descriptions to the *Los Angeles Times*, that is, the *Sunday Magazine*, during 1899–1900, in addition to some poetry.) It appears that after Helen's arrival both Gelett Burgess and the journalists Will and Wallace Irwin had encouraged Nora to write and sell short stories, in addition to her poems, as a supplement to her usual salary. Both Burgess and the Irwin brothers must have seen some representative examples of Nora's prose, become impressed, and urged her to augment her income in a more practical way than with the isolated lyric poems she managed to sell to either local or national magazines.

Apart from their dealings with the San Francisco Bohemians—many of whom had become true friends at least with Nora, but about whom Helen increasingly came to have ambiguous feelings—the life that the sisters led while working in downtown San Francisco and residing in the cottage on Lombard Street afforded them many pleasant occasions together, especially on the weekends, when they both apparently had not only Sunday but also part of Saturday to themselves. They reserved specifically for themselves their Saturday afternoons. Taking the ferries when suitable, the young women searched San Francisco, Berkeley, and Oakland for beautiful and uncommon objects from the Far East, such as fabrics, pieces of clothing like kimonos, Japanese and Chinese prints, and so forth. They both felt keenly the allure of the exotic Orient.

For Nora such a search paralleled that animating much of her poetry, the quest for the beauty that endures, thus a very personal or individual quest. The sisters often took the ferry to Marin County, the peninsula to the north similar to the one occupied by the City, to such places as Tiburon and Sausalito. Sometimes they traveled to Muir Woods, a favorite ambiance of tranquility with its towering redwoods and sheltering umbrage, where they would talk, walk, and re-create themselves. Helen recalls Nora and herself—decked out in Pendleton-style shirts, jodhpurs with leggings, and sturdy, practical shoes—striding over the grassy and then mostly undeveloped hills of Sausalito. Such afternoons became their preferred moments of dreaming and reverie together. In the evening they returned to the City, usually to meet with a number of the Bohemian crowd of artists and writers.

The spring of 1907, probably around June, emerged as a time of festivities for a number of their Bohemian friends. Gelett Burgess and the Irwin brothers decided to pursue careers as freelance writers in New York City. Xavier Martinez married his Elsie, and Porter Garnett also got married. Nora wrote the charming and somewhat admonitory sonnet "The Rose" as a gift for her printer friend. The relationship between Lafler and Nora May had its ups and downs, and he did not always find her an ideal companion, given that her periods of happiness alternated with those of intense depression, as pointed out by Joanne Lafler. Although Nora often hid her hypersensitivity under a mask of bantering or lighthearted mockery, she did not hesitate to play one beau against the other, since she was also seeing Captain Hiley, her other suitor. However, Lafler evidently felt secure enough to continue his relationship with Nora, whatever other problems they may have had.

Separated from his wife Alice Sherrill since September 1904 and eager to solidify his relationship with Nora May, Harry now took the initiative into his own hands. According to Joanne Lafler, he filed for divorce on 5 August 1907. If his suit succeeded, following the final decree, he would then be able to legitimize his relationship with Nora by marrying her. However, he had not known, or fully reckoned with, her almost pathological distaste for marriage. She would have none of it, and this must have proven quite a shock to Harry. Sometime between early and late August that same summer, Nora terminated her liaison with Lafler, and the two lovers parted for good. Helen and Nora quit their jobs, broke up the household on Lombard Street, packed up and headed south, Helen going on to Los Angeles and Nora to follow her after a visit with the Sterlings in Carmel. By early September, Nora had already taken up again with the dashing Captain Hiley, who came down to Carmel from his lumber ranch north of Santa Cruz.

George Sterling had become increasingly concerned about Nora May's health—she never appeared robust in any way—and was fearful that she was overtasking what little strength she had by working all day and writing at night. George had by this time come to regard her as a very dear sister, and as one even dearer to him than those of his own blood. The Sterlings had invited her to Carmel for an extended visit, seemingly open-ended. A special point: In the course of his preeminence on the West Coast, say, during 1903–26, Sterling helped as many fellow poets and fellow writers as his circumstances allowed—bespeaking a true nobility of character—but of all the persons he helped, his direct, personal assistance to Nora May French must count as the single most significant example until his encounter and friendship with Clark Ashton Smith during 1911–26.

Late in August, Nora accepted the Sterlings' invitation and moved to Carmel, initially to spend no more than a couple of weeks there. Helen at least had become disenchanted with San Francisco's as well as Carmel's Bohemians, even if Nora herself continued to like them. Helen did have both respect and affection for the Sterlings. The sisters had obviously come to some kind of agreement. But once Nora settled in at Carmel, for whatever causes, she seemed to be drifting at random or had become undecided. Maybe she would simply stay there for awhile, indefinitely.

Meanwhile things external to the insular affairs of Northern California's Bohemia had moved forward, whereby Sterling passed from a California figure known only locally to one who became not just nationally but even internationally celebrated. Bierce had at last secured publication for Sterling's locally renowned poem "A Wine of Wizardry." That summer of 1907 a new editor had taken the helm of the *Cosmopolitan Magazine*, one of the holdings of William Randolph Hearst, and at Bierce's urging Sam Chamberlain bought the poem. It appeared in the issue for September, accompanied by Bierce's trenchant article "A Poet and His Poem," in which Sterling's mentor did not hesitate to praise in the highest possible terms the outré narrative in verse. Chamberlain presented the poem in gorgeous fashion with elegant art nouveau decorations by F. I. Bennett, and preceded the actual text with a provocative heading:

> Mr. James Bryce, author of "The American Commonwealth," and British ambassador to the United States, in a widely quoted interview implied that this country lacked poets. The Cosmopolitan offers the following remarkable poem as proof that there is at least one poet in America. Mr. Ambrose Bierce discusses the verses in another part of this issue. Obviously Mr. Bryce had not read Mrs. Ella Wheeler Wilcox's splendid poem, "Abelard and Heloise."

The poem, with this heading and as critically presented and judiciously commended by Bierce, inspired a delightful tempest of controversy, the net result of which made his poet pupil almost a household name. Sterling henceforth became a recognized figure and a poetic authority in his own right. It remained the best piece of critical good fortune to befall the poet. Bierce loved a good fight (not surprisingly, given his military record in the Civil War), and he took on all the critics of Sterling and himself in another article about the poem, "An Insurrection of the Peasantry," published in the December issue of the *Cosmopolitan*. Editor Chamberlain and owner Hearst solidly supported the controversy, of course: it helped sell his magazine, but Chamberlain had nonetheless rendered a real service to American literature, and poetry in particular, by publishing both Sterling's poem and Bierce's two essays.

The redoubtable Mary Austin and Nora May finally met in person at Carmel, and in spite of whatever differences they may have had, they became good friends and confided in each other, as had Helen and Nora. Many years later, in her autobiography *Earth Horizon* (1932)—when discussing "the liability of men of genius to find their subjective activities on their way to fruition so largely at the mercy of the effect on them of women"—Mary paid Nora a great compliment: "I never needed a love affair to release the subconscious in me, nor did Nora May French, who was the only other woman of our circle whose gifts approached Sterling's or London's."

Nevertheless, once she resumed her liaison with Captain Alan Hiley, Nora seemed quite content. Even though still married like Lafler, Alan came down to Carmel in mid-September to spend a weekend visit with Nora. Evidently the two considered themselves promised to each other in some sense. In a letter written after that weekend to her friend Blanche Partington, as quoted by Judith Allen in her thesis, Carrie Sterling gives us the following valuable report:

> Nora May French has been here two weeks with intervals. She sleeps in the tent house and gets her breakfast in town and sometimes other meals—so I find her no trouble and like her ever so much. She is an odd monkey, but is awfully bright. Her "man," as she calls him, came here last Saturday and stayed until Monday. He has a timber farm up in the Santa Cruz Mountains about six miles from Santa Cruz. He's an [expatriate] Englishman. His name is Captain Alan Ille-Hiley—and has as a guardian Sir something Marlshon of England.

He is a dandy fellow—intelligent and modest—calls himself "Mr. Hiley." We all liked him immensely and are glad she is going to marry so fine a fellow—in the spring.—Her sister will also marry in the spring. Nora May has shipped Lafler which is a good thing I believe.—They were not suited in any way.

The Sterlings encouraged Nora to continue living with them, and thus the original couple of weeks became a couple of months. Although now settled at Carmel, or so it seemed, Nora still took the train on occasion to Oakland and San Francisco, from which she would bring back to Carrie news of their mutual friends. Both the Sterlings and Nora seemed content with their living arrangements, they in their bungalow and she in her cabin or tent-house alongside the bungalow. While sojourning with the Sterlings, Nora could now do all or most of the things she formerly loved to do while in Southern California. An ardent and not unskilled horsewoman, she loved to go for extended rides on horseback, just like her heroine Dolores in "The Spanish Girl."

Meanwhile in mid-October the *Saturday Evening Post* published Nora's semi-autobiographical story "The Diary of a Telephone Girl." Although Gelett Burgess had kindly supplied a few finishing touches, the story firmly remains Nora's own creation. The sale and publication not only meant much to Nora—she could always use the money—but it also impressed her friends in San Francisco and now Carmel as a major step forward in her career as a professional writer. It is a shame that circumstances did not allow Nora to follow it up with further substantial fiction.

Otherwise life in Carmel went on in a pleasant and stimulating way for the Sterlings and for Nora living by their side. Helen was expecting her sister to return at any time to live with her in Los Angeles and to continue her writing career there in Southern California, rather than in the rootless and hedonistic Bohemian circles of Carmel and San Francisco. Nora seemed undecided as to when she would leave, and at least the Sterlings expected her to stay through the winter in Carmel. All appeared to be going well, and early in November Carrie wrote to Blanche Partington, as quoted by Judith Allen in her thesis: "Nora May is in her coop and at work," then adding that "we are going to build a tiny kitchen on it where she will be comfy for the winter [. . .]. Nora May was saying how she'd love to have you bunk with her this winter."

Nora greatly enjoyed the frequent gatherings of artists and writers, which she attended whether they occurred on the beach, in the woods, in some open meadow, or at someone's rustic dwelling. Sometime in 1905 or 1906, during the course of their mussel and abalone feasts, Sterling began creating what became a celebrated song, evidently actually sung, although no one seems to have noted or notated the existent melody, whether expressly composed, or adapted from a pre-existing source. This was the "Abalone Song," conceived in a rollicking ballad metre, a basic poetic form that almost anyone can master. To this famous ditty it seems that almost everyone among the Bohemians contributed something. With her proven skill for humorous verse, Nora certainly would have contributed one or more stanzas.

Only one dissonant episode occurred to mar the Arcadian idyll, and for Nora specifically. This happened during her sojourn at Carmel, on Sunday, 2 September, at one of the afternoon gatherings of the Carmel Bohemians. Nora happened to fall. She hit her head hard on some rock, and it evidently hurt quite a bit, since she continued to weep throughout the rest of that afternoon. Of course, everyone became concerned, and the accident naturally disturbed several individuals, especially Sterling himself. Nora recovered from the immediate pain, but the physical hurt may have left some residual damage, resulting in her later disequilibration and intensified suicidal mood.

As everyone recalled later who had socialized with her during the last two weeks of her life, the first two weeks of November 1907, Nora talked of suicide over and over. It seems she was harboring certain tensions that she apparently did not discuss with anyone there in Carmel, but may have mentioned to her sister Helen. Evidently she had consummated physically her love with Captain Hiley. We can only speculate, but it is possible that Nora was pregnant again, and this time by Hiley, necessitating another abortion. However, given her frequent lack of vitality, and given that she may have already had one or more abortions, Nora might have found herself reluctant to have another.

But Nora was harboring other tensions as well, or so it would seem. According to several witnesses who nonetheless do not appear to have consulted with her directly, Nora had fallen in love with the writer and fictioneer Jimmy Hopper, with whom she had often socialized while sojourning in Carmel, along with the Sterlings. Jimmy was living there with Fred Bechdolt, and his wife and children still resided in the Bay Area. Furthermore, Jimmy, George, and Nora often met on the beach behind Jimmy's bungalow to share their latest writings, often reading them aloud, and then discussing them during that autumn twilight. It made a pleasant way to end the daylight hours. Hopper certainly did like Nora as woman and poet, and he did exhibit care and kindness to her. Nora might have loved and admired Hopper as man and writer, but not romantically. However, none of that means, as averred or adumbrated by some individuals then or since, that she had become infatuated with him, that she tried to tell him of her love, but that he, not understanding, acted only nonplussed at this confession, and that she then perceived this response as outright rejection. Presumably this rejection may have contributed to the reasons for her suicide.

(Even more fantastic, according to Joseph Noel in his memoir *Footloose in Arcadia* [1940], Nora—reacting to what she felt was rejection—then actually tried to poison Jimmy. Such an action does not accord in any fashion with what we know concerning Nora's life and character.)

It does not seem likely that Nora would have committed suicide because of either a romantic infatuation or a simple rejection. She was a woman who could have had as lover almost any man she might have desired (according to Sterling, in a letter to Bierce dated 8 February 1908, "she played with men as with pebbles"). Nora had written in pencil a kind of prose-poem, "The Suicide," which she gave to Hopper, possibly during the last two weeks of her life. Sometime after her death certain friends must have told Jimmy the rumor that Nora had fallen in love with him, but feeling that he had rejected her, had then killed herself. Sterling himself did not credit the story. Even if Hopper did not rationally credit the rumor, he still brooded on both her suicide and the prose-poem, and he kept it among his papers until his death, after which at some point his family gave these papers to the Bancroft Library.

Until the publication of Nora's poems in 1910, Jimmy felt guilty for her death in a sense but, as it emerged, without just cause. Despite the coincidence, the prose-poem demonstrates that the thought of suicide weighed heavily on her mind during those last two weeks, if not longer. Recalling Nora's death many years later, but indicating other causes for her suicide than unrequited love for Jimmy Hopper, Mary Austin corroborates Nora's obsession with suicide in She writes in *Earth Horizon*: "Nora May was ill and troubled. She was in debt and unable to make a living. She talked of suicide. As a matter of fact she contrived it the next night after I left Carmel. She could not afford to live. George scattered her ashes on Point Lobos." (Austin's memory is at fault here. She actually left Carmel on 2 November, twelve days before Nora's death by suicide.)

Whatever the cause or causes—depression, pregnancy, lack of good health, despair from poverty or at being in debt, unrequited love—Nora did succeed at committing suicide, although she had to try more than once. Not quite mid-month, without George's knowledge, she borrowed his revolver, and going out on some woodland path not far away, she tried to shoot herself, but the bullet only snipped off a tress of her hair. Something had happened to spoil her aim, and she did not pursue the matter further. Nora returned to the house, where the Sterlings awaited her, having noted the absence of the revolver. She casually handed him the tress thus clipped off at the same time that she returned his weapon, explaining what had happened. She had lost her high resolve at the last moment, and this loss had spoiled her aim. Nora then declared that this attempt had cured her of any desire to commit suicide. Possibly the Sterlings thought that she was joking, because neither noted any powder marks on her hair, either on the tress or on her head.

Nora would try suicide again. On the morning of 13 November, she bought a quantity of a poison, cyanide of potassium, from the local doctor and pharmacist in Carmel, one Dr. Beck, saying that she wanted to use it to clean some silver, a known application for the chemical. George departed that evening to go to Oakland on some business, leaving Carrie and Nora behind in the bungalow. Nora slept that night inside the house so that she and Carrie could keep each other company. During that evening at some point Nora confided to Carrie how disillusioned she had become with life and with men. Sleeping in the main bedroom usually shared by George and Carrie, they went to bed early, that night of the 13th, around 10 o'clock, but resting in separate beds with a small table between. Carrie noted that Nora seemed especially cheerful, and so they both went to sleep.

Sometime just before midnight the creaking of the bathroom door awoke Carrie, who called out, and Nora responded that she was getting a drink of water. Carrie specifically noted that the clock struck midnight just as the bathroom door made the noise that awoke her. Sterling's wife heard Nora pour a glass and then return to the bedroom to lie down on the other bed. Nora had apparently taken the cyanide with the glass of water as quietly as possible so as not to call Carrie's attention to what she was doing. A few seconds later Carrie heard a strange noise coming from Nora's throat, evidently the death rattle. Sterling's wife got up and, striking a match, lit the lamp. Nora lay stiff on the bed, foam at her lips. The foam disappeared, the rattle stopped, her face became normal, and then pale. For the next hour or so Carrie tried unsuccessfully to revive Nora. She put moistened towels around her head and sat on the bed until she felt chilled. Then, finding Nora cold, she got into bed with her, trying to warm her, when she noticed the white sediment in the glass on the table between the beds. She got up out of bed and ran to look in a medical book in the library.

Before she left Carmel, Mary Austin had been writing a novel in which the heroine kills herself with cyanide of potassium. Carrie suddenly recalled how Nora had asked Mary all about the poison and its effects. Finally becoming frightened and putting on a wrap, Carrie ran out of the house and went to Jimmy Hopper's place, where the writer Fred Bechdolt was also living, collaborating with Jimmy on a writing project. The two men got out of bed at once when Carrie knocked. After she explained what had happened, Jimmy went to fetch Dr. Beck, and Fred returned with Carrie to her home. By the time Jimmy arrived with the doctor and the latter examined the body, everyone understood that Nora had died. Thus gathered together, the group spent the rest of the night telegraphing friends and relatives, Helen and Edward French in Los Angeles, George Sterling in Oakland, Captain Hiley in the Santa Cruz Mountains, Henry Lafler in San Francisco, among others.

Everybody convened as soon as possible, most of them the very next day. The next morning, 14 November, at 11 o'clock, Coroner Muller appeared, enrolled a jury, and listened to the evidence given by Carrie, Jimmy, Fred, and the physician. The inquest took place in the afternoon. When Carrie testified, the jury wept openly. After the inquest Jimmy Hopper took it upon himself to inform the San Francisco press, probably by telegraph, concerning the main facts of Nora's death along with salient details. According to Carrie, the *San Francisco Examiner* for 15 November 1907 featured the most accurate account, under the headline "Midnight Lure of Death Leads Poetess to Grave. " Near the end the article revealed a poignant piece of news about an extraordinary event that some friends must have arranged on Nora's behalf, whereby she would have made her public début reading her own poems in posh surroundings: "San Francisco society was to have seen and heard her on Thanksgiving eve, when she was to have read at the Fairmont. But instead of the applause and compliments of society she preferred the grave and the great poetic silences."

Later that same day, after the inquest, as quoted by Judith Allen in her thesis, Carrie wrote a letter to Blanche Partington, to reassure her friend that she was coping with the tragedy. She not only pays Nora a substantial compliment, but discloses unequivocally how much she loved her.

... The Examiner account is just about perfect as to facts (as Hopper gave them) so I will not write about it. I feel she is happier, so why be selfish and wish it undone—If she chose this place to die in I am sure I do not mind and the atmosphere will be sweeter with her parting breath—It was hard to go thro' but it's past and I am so old, oh so old and wise—

I loved Nora May, and she told me the night she died that I and her sister were the only two women who had loved and been kind to her. I think that we did everything to make her happy and she was I am sure but the worm was at the bud and she couldn't overcome it. Dear child—I find a gold hair pin, a *wad* of *gum* stuck in some wall, and bits of her trinkets here and there which still remind me that she was here so full of fun and wit but two days ago. She played the game—she died looking so beautiful. . . . She chose to die among those she loved, and she did it as beautifully as it could have been done, such a girl . . . she was so big and brave.

Many years later, in an oral history, Elsie Whitaker Martinez would recall some of what Carrie told her sometime after the suicide, of what Carrie had remembered from the conversation exchanged between Nora and herself on 13 November 1907, that final evening in the life of the young poet. As noted elsewhere, Nora hid her extreme sensitivity (not to mention her passionate nature) under a mask of bantering, of lighthearted mockery. Apparently she disclosed her true feelings to very few people, such as her sister Helen, or Mary Austin, or Carrie Sterling. That final night Nora May confessed to Carrie that she had become disillusioned with life and with men, but without adding, of course, that she had become disillusioned enough to end her existence.

True, George at least had been half expecting Nora's death by suicide, but even then, upon his return to Carmel from Oakland, he seemed ill with shock and sorrow. However, once it happened, he became resigned to the fact. He, too, had loved Nora, no less than had Carrie. The unconventional funeral that unfurled about a week later took place in complete accordance with Nora's wishes. According to Michael Williams, she had left a note stating her wishes in regard to the disposal of her body. She had wanted her ashes dispersed into the Pacific Ocean from a favorite spot on Cypress Point or on Point Lobos. Her friends carried out her final wishes exactly as she had specified. They had her body cremated at a funeral establishment with a crematorium in San Francisco. Apparently not knowing that all went forward according to her own wishes, the funeral plans shocked some of Nora's relatives on the East Coast, particularly an uncle in Brooklyn, a Presbyterian minister, who had exercised a strong influence on her in her childhood. He had ostentatiously refused to send any money to finance the "heathen ceremony."

An historical aside: Monterey possessed the railroad station closest to Carmel, and the most convenient place whether to go north to San Francisco or south to Los Angeles. Nora's friends, probably Sterling or Hopper, drove over with horse and wagon carrying her cadaver to Monterey from Carmel. Shipping the body north to the City by the Golden Gate as the most convenient place with a full funeral establishment and crematorium, Sterling himself probably accompanied the corpse on Friday, 15 November, up to San Francisco, where George had the body cremated the next day. With the ashes enshrined in the usual utilitarian urn, George then returned to Carmel via Monterey on Monday, 18 November, on the morning train. All was ready for the ceremony scheduled for that afternoon.

It seems that Nora had enjoyed more than one favorite spot to which she would ride on horseback in order to meditate or contemplate. One was Cypress Point, facing the Pacific Ocean on the seventeen-mile drive at the western edge of the Monterey peninsula; another preferred locale, a promontory somewhere on the granite cliffs of Point Lobos also looking out over the ocean. After announcing that the ceremony would go forward at Cypress Point sometime on 18 November—that is, the scattering of Nora's ashes into the sea highlighted by a short and simple ritual—her friends and family withdrew the announcement and postponed the event. Subsequently, without any public announcement, they rearranged it for Friday, 22 November, and moved the event from Cypress Point to the new location on the granite cliffs at the western edge of Point Lobos. Apparently the friends and family did this in order to avoid publicity, to exclude the merely curious, or any idle sensation-seekers, and thus to include only those who had known and genuinely cared for Nora while she was alive.

On a clear and beautiful day during latter autumn, 22 November 1907, family and friends gathered at the new location on the seaward cliffs that rise up at the edge of the extensive land mass known as Point Lobos, which lies to the south of Carmel. Each friend read a personal composition as a tribute to the deceased poet. Sister Helen and Captain Hiley performed the ceremony, and then George Sterling as the elder poet in the group scattered her ashes from the funeral urn into the ocean, assisted by Lafler and Hiley as her two most conspicuous lovers. After the ceremony the usual visiting and socializing would have taken place, most likely at the Sterlings' bungalow. The beautiful and simple obsequies had apparently gone forward in a dignified and worthy manner, perhaps more evocative of Graeco-Roman antiquity than anything else.

Some of those people attending the obsequies from afar may have lingered an extra day or so, but within a few days many leading Bohemians departed from Carmel. Mary Austin had already left twelve days before Nora's death; now Helen and Edward French returned to Los Angeles, and Captain Hiley returned to his timber farm that might have become Nora May's future home. Genuinely grief-stricken, Lafler went back to his editing in San Francisco. James Hopper departed with his family for the East Coast to pursue his literary career in New York City, where his writing in fact would prosper and the sale of his fiction to the national magazines would meet success, establishing him as one of the better and better-known short-story writers of that period. Despite success Hopper would remain homesick for California and Carmel, to which he would return but at a much later date. Soon the Sterlings remained by themselves in Carmel, where they would spend the winter of 1907–08.

At long last the whole sad affair of Nora May French had ended. The curious and otherwise unresolved suspense of her last days and her tragic suicide had formed a source of grief and profound shock that would linger in Carmel and haunt the area for an extended period, to say nothing of its impact on Nora May's immediate family, Helen and Edward French. For sister Helen in particular the shock of that loss not only would linger for many years to come, but would trouble her the rest of her life.

Sterling wrote to his mentor and master Bierce a long and extraordinary letter dated 7 December 1907, in which he mentions Nora May several times. He had already sent him a copy of the *San Francisco Examiner* for 15 November 1907 that featured the long and tastefully sensationalistic article about Nora May's death and its immediate aftermath. Now he reports: "Nov. 22nd we cast her ashes into the sea from her favorite cliff at Point Carmel [Point Lobos]." Then, as he goes on to give Bierce a capsule portrait of her, he pays her a high compliment:

> Someday I will tell you all about her. She was a wonderful girl, heedless of fame, luxury, companionship and most of the things on which most of us set our hearts. An inscrutable creature, with hair of the brightest gold and a deadly smile (her lips *were* like "a scarlet thread"), she has made me feel

small as a gnat, and my friends nearly as small, by her suicide. Living seems in bad taste, now that she is dead.

No scandal attended her going out, nor was she enceinte, though she had several lovers. But she was a stormy petrel, and left pain in her wake.

Her death has made Carmel, and our home, more beautiful than ever to us, because she did us the honor of dying in my house. And it has brought Carrie and me very near together.

The whole sad affair of the Golden Girl—as Jimmy Hopper had already named her with a touch of poetry before her death—had ended, but the aftermath, involving above all the publication of her poems, had only begun.

III

Following the death and obsequies of Nora May French, the effects of the immediate aftermath did not subside at once, but continued to echo for some time, not just in the San Francisco press, but also in contemporary periodicals, Californian or otherwise. In the issue for Saturday, 23 November, of *Town Talk* (the San Francisco equivalent of the *New Yorker*), editor-in-chief Theodore F. Bonnet discussed at some length Nora's tragic end in the regular department "The Spectator" (an unsigned column usually written by Bonnet in full or in part). However, judging from the rather unsympathetic remarks on such of her poetry as had seen publication in magazines up to that moment, the editor or staff writer showed no real discernment into what makes Nora's work stand out in terms of genuine individuality and originality.

At least the poet's hometown had not forgotten her. The *Los Angeles Times* proved far more sympathetic and succinct than *Town Talk* in a series of brief articles, each an "Exclusive Dispatch" sent "By Direct Wire to the Times," in the successive issues for 15, 17, and 18 November. The article that appeared on the 17th mentions that Nora suffered from "an organic disease," a phrase probably supplied by her family. If a genuine report and not a euphemism for pregnancy, this fact adds considerably to our understanding of what may have led to Nora's taking her own life.

Although they would entrain for the San Francisco Bay Area every now and then, the Sterlings for the most part remained by themselves in Carmel. Even if they felt honored that the Golden Girl had chosen their home in which to die, both George and Carrie also felt haunted by the unexplained mystery and tragedy of Nora May's suicide. For George this haunting found expression in several poetic tributes, and he also became, willy-nilly, the receptor or focus of other poetic tributes and elegies to Nora's memory, as revealed in his correspondence with Bierce and others that winter and later. In a letter dated 8 February 1908, Sterling indicates that he has written a tribute to her, a sonnet, but also includes a second sonnet that Lafler created after seeing her body laid out after her death. This piece by Lafler therefore ranks as the first memorial poem to Nora written by anyone.

Somewhat later Lafler wrote another, much longer tribute—"The Pearl." In contains over 140 lines, and Sterling found it particularly beautiful. He mentions it several times as such in letters or in print. Lafler redacted this distinctly magical poem the year after Nora May's death, and it made its first appearance in *Sunset* in the issue for October 1908. Remarkable for its abbreviated lines, its apparently exotic subject, and its mesmerizingly sustained quality, "The Pearl" ranks as the first piece of poetic homage to Nora published anywhere, even if Lafler cites neither her name nor her initials.

In a letter to Bierce dated 26 February 1908, Sterling encloses his own second sonnet honoring her memory, the superb tribute "Nora May French," which he included in his second collection of poetry, *A Wine of Wizardry and Other Poems*, published by A. M. Robertson in 1909. Still haunted by her death and its mystery, sometime between 1909 and 1911 Sterling created a third tribute to her memory, "The Ashes in the Sea: N.M.F.," which he included in his third volume of poetry, *The House of Orchids and Other Poems*, published by A. M. Robertson in 1911. This final tribute in verse ranks as possibly his most poignant of them all, especially the final stanza, which he oddly deleted for the poem's inclusion in his volume of *Selected Poems*, published by Henry Holt in 1923.

Around this time, something much more important than any prose or poetic tributes to her memory (although they contributed to the lore and legends already growing around that very memory) went forward—the preparation for publication of Nora's unique volume of poetry, under the primary care of Sterling himself with Lafler and Porter Garnett as his equal partners. Either in person at the time of Nora's unorthodox funeral, or later in correspondence, Sterling would have discussed the publication of Nora's poems with Helen and Edward French as a matter of first importance and even urgency. From Jimmy Hopper's letter to Sterling dated sometime in April 1909 (Helen French Hunt also confirmed this in person to the present writer), we know that Nora's sister (speaking on behalf of both her father and herself) had left the matter in Sterling's hands "a year and a half ago" (in Hopper's own phrase), that is, at the time of the obsequies, or shortly thereafter, in late November or early December 1907.

Nora's death had still caught many people by surprise, especially her sister and her father, as well as her friends and any other relatives whether in Southern California or elsewhere. Much later, during the early 1960s, in response to inquiries from Judith Allen concerning the possibility that additional manuscripts and letters had survived, Helen French Hunt made the following strategic statement in a letter written sometime in February 1963.

> The tempest and tragedy of Nora's last year, coupled with unhappy incidents in my own life, blurred a period when I should have collected her effects and mss. Her father and I probably shared her own conviction that her early work was not too important; that it would mature and strengthen when the difficult . . . period passed. It's hard to realize now. But we did give constant encouragement and appreciation.

As we have learned, Helen was to have married some unspecified person that same spring when Nora May and Captain Hiley were also to have married, at least according to Nora. Apparently this marriage of Helen's did not take place; she did marry a few years later, but whether to the same person to whom she had been engaged earlier is unclear. Busy with their own lives, neither family nor friends could have known that in Nora's case the early writing, along with what she managed to accomplish in her last years, would constitute her only surviving work.

Be that as it may, since her sister and her father had left the matter in Sterling's hands, George naturally turned to Lafler as the logical, if not the only real, source as the guardian of her poems as well as of any and all information relating to the poems. George had some poems and some information, especially as left behind by the poet among her effects in the little cabin where she had lived from September to November 1907, but he would have pooled all this with what Lafler possessed. As a result of the long and extensive correspondence between Nora and himself (spring 1905–summer 1907), Lafler held the major part of the poems or knew the most about them. Porter Garnett must have offered his expert services as a fine printer or (rather) typesetter at the outset as a close friend of both Sterling and Lafler. Thus united, they managed to have the volume ready by the late spring of 1910. Indeed, Sterling could make this report to Bierce in his letter dated 24 November:

> We have Miss French's poems nearly read for the printer—I've had to read proofs for the last two days. [. . .] The more I read her poems, the finer

they seem to me, the purer, the more poignant. Take, for an instance, the end of the enclosed sonnet: to me it conveys an almost overwhelming sense of the tragic, the unearthly, the—I don't know what. Perhaps I'm hypnotized; but all my poet-friends agree with me, so it would have to be "collective hallucination."

The volume, with the front cover simply imprinted with *Poems* at the top and *Nora May French* at the bottom, made its official appearance in June 1910. Recognized by this time as an art printer of national reputation, Garnett had beautifully set the entire volume by hand, all 74 poems, but the Stanley-Taylor Company of San Francisco did the actual printing, on thick Italian paper, each copy bound between boards in silver-gray cloth or "vellum-backed wood-veneer boards." It is probable that others beside the original three contributed to the cost of production, especially Jack London. The copyright page reads: "Copyright 1910, / By the Strange Company." Of course, this represents Garnett, Lafler, and Sterling. Whoever contributed to the cost of production did not lose money on the venture, even if such a thought would have played little or no part in the calculations of those involved in the volume's preparation.

The tipped-in frontispiece features a striking but unsmiling portrait of Nora by Arnold Genthe, with her full signature reproduced in facsimile underneath the photograph. Altogether, the volume represents a little masterpiece of tasteful Art Nouveau book design and production. Nora May's friends had achieved a superb tribute in honor of her touching and unique poetry—an act of piety beautifully done. In Genthe's photographic portrait, although simply dressed, Nora looks the very embodiment of the feminine ideal as imaged and adored by the Pre-Raphaelite artists and poets in England of the latter nineteenth century. This archetypal or iconic resemblance appears uniquely pertinent, inasmuch as Xavier Martinez and other (mostly Northern) Californian artists of the late nineteenth and early twentieth centuries—famous for their landscapes, murals, and portraits—also have their obvious affinities with the English Pre-Raphaelites.

According to Judith Allen, "The publication of Nora May French's *Poems* elicited a good deal of attention in the local press. Several articles appeared which included selections of her work, a brief résumé of her life, and some of the several Arnold Genthe photographs. Poetess Ina Coolbrith saved a clipping in the back of her copy of *Poems* which contained one of the few articles which attempted to deal critically with the poetry." ["Newspaper clipping from an unidentified newspaper June 16, 1910, to be found in the Ina Coolbrith copy of *Poems* . . . in the Bancroft Library of the University of California, Berkeley."]

Whatever else they may have represented, these articles did not constitute regular reviews. Apparently the three people making up the Strange Company, for whatever the reason, sent out few review copies—whether to the local or the national press—and the one regular review that we have, from the *New Age* (published in London), from the issue of Thursday, 14 July 1910, apparently came about by happenstance. The person who wrote it, Michael Williams, managed to obtain a copy (by purchase or as gift) and penned his account of it on his own recognizance, and not in response to any solicitation by the publishers. The article "Van de Landen van Over-Zee" by Hein Boeken (followed by his own sonnet "God en Sater"), which appeared in *De Nieuwe Gids* for November 1910, seems to be more of an impressionistic reverie based on Nora's book rather than an orthodox review (although it does contain faint echoes from her life and poetry), and exists in a class of its own. The edition of 500 copies became exhausted soon after its appearance, not only because of the notoriety associated with Nora's dramatic demise but even more because of the poetry's intrinsic merits.

On the other hand, given the lack of regular reviews, the individual responses to the little volume, wherever chronicled, proved exceptionally vivid and significant. Still residing and working back in New York City, Jimmy Hopper sent Sterling a letter written sometime in July 1910, in which he details an individual but sympathetic reaction to the poetry; what is more, he makes a profound observation about Nora's hypersensitivity, which resulted on the one hand in her exquisite poetry but on the other hand in the conclusion, or so Jimmy surmises, that much of life must have seemed like pure torture for her in everyday circumstances. If his insight has validity, then it constitutes further and even more compelling evidence as to why she committed suicide. We quote from Jimmy's letter here as cited by Judith Allen in her thesis.

> I have Nora May's poems. I've looked through several times, reading here and there. The damn trouble is that when I do so, I hear her voice. At the same time—contradictory as it may seem—the reading fortifies a feeling I had and had lost—that of reconciliation to her death. To that girl many moments of living must have been simple torture. Her poetry was a vampire

feeding upon her; and some of her best things are floating gossamers the strands of which are bleeding heartshreds.

I am not surprised at all that Ambrose Bierce should not care much for the poems. Nora May was essentially lyric, and he is everything but lyric. He is absolutely objective. He, objective and sculptural.

But as we now know, Bierce actually had a better opinion of Nora as a poet than what at first might appear. That year, 1910, proved notable for one other event in the French family. A large expatriate community of English natives had grown up in the general Pasadena area of Southern California, similar to the one that had established itself in and around Santa Monica, that is, on the coast or the general west side of the Los Angeles basin. Nora's sister had met an Englishman in Pasadena, one Charles D. Hunt, with whom she fell in love, and with whom she could share such a life as her parents had enjoyed (but had eluded Nora), including music, art, literature, and long rambling walks. This could be the same individual whom Helen had planned to marry during the spring of 1908, at the same time as Nora May and Captain Hiley might have married, had not certain problems arisen to prevent Helen's marriage at that time. The marriage between Charles and Helen took place, but because of certain difficulties that came about during their first year of marriage, they agreed on a trial separation of six months while they could each discover, and put in order, their individual emotional priorities. The separation succeeded, Charles and Helen began living together again, and indeed went on to enjoy many years of satisfying and happy marriage.

Both husband and wife apparently worked, and they bought and maintained a beautiful home amid beautiful natural surroundings in one of the canyon areas of Pasadena. Here they would often entertain their friends and relatives, especially from among the members of the area's large expatriate English community. They had no children, but managed to lead a full and successful existence until the husband's death sometime in the 1960s. After his death, Helen sold their property and moved into an apartment in South Pasadena, where she would reside until her death in 1973. Over the years both Charles and Helen would often travel to Northern California (among other destinations) to sojourn or vacation in and around the same places where Helen and Nora had once done the same thing in the San Francisco Bay Area, Carmel, and Monterey. Besides living her own and generally successful existence, Helen managed to preserve much information about her poet sister's brief life, as well as selected personal effects of hers. In addition, over the years—that is, from 1907 until Carrie Sterling's death in August 1918 and George's death in November 1926—Helen kept in touch on occasion with the Sterlings, sometimes by letter, but more often through personal visits when Charles and Helen found themselves in the Bay Area.

Nineteen years after her death, during the summer of 1926, Sterling paid Nora May French one final tribute in public, but this time in prose. One of the last works of real significance that he wrote is his account of Californian poetry for William Stanley Braithwaite's *Anthology of Magazine Verse* for 1926, published in late 1926 by Harold Vinal of Boston. Put together evidently between late June and early August of that year, this account, "The Poetry of the Pacific Coast—California," appears along with other accounts dealing with the poetry of other sectors of the United States but before the anthology's main text. Here, toward the end of his article, Sterling devotes an entire paragraph to Nora May French and her work. But before that paragraph, while mentioning and appraising various poets and other figures—such contemporaries as Herman George Scheffauer, Henry Anderson Lafler, Porter Garnett, and Gelett Burgess—Sterling evokes the already long-vanished fin-de-siècle of 1900 with its immediate aftermath, that older Bohemia before its extension during 1905 and later into Carmel by means of Sterling himself: "My recollection conjures up again the twilight period of the last and the present century, those days of San Francisco's old Bohemian repute, 'before the fire and earthquake'" of 1906.

How many memories must have come flocking back to the unofficial poet laureate of the West Coast while he was writing this account of a world that had vanished as irretrievably as ancient Atlantis beneath the waves!

> And first in memory of those days that already begin to take on the royal purple of distance comes the magical one of the beautiful Nora May French. She was born in western New York, but came to Los Angeles when still a child. Not long after our great fire she came to San Francisco, and was the most charming personage of the group of Bohemians that foregathered at Coppa's restaurant, then in San Francisco's most romantic building, the Montgomery Block. She died in the following year (November 13, 1907), leaving behind her poems (published later by her fiancé, Henry Anderson Lafler), of singularly limpid beauty. She had been influenced mainly by Tennyson and Housman: hence the blending in her poetry of a fine simplicity, sincere emotion, and crystalline workmanship. She would, had she lived,

have been perhaps the first woman poet of America. Her sonnet, "The Outer Gate," is one of the most quietly terrible ones in our literature.

Almost at once after this especial remembrance, Sterling devotes a paragraph or so to his own chief protégé (that is, after Nora herself), carefully tempering his appraisal so as not to seem too laudatory.

> A younger and immensely imaginative singer is Clark Ashton Smith, the story of whose triumph with his neighbors, when hundreds of copies of his first book of verses were promptly bought up in a small California hill town, is a romance in itself. He is the author of *The Star-Treader*, *Odes and Sonnets*, *Ebony and Crystal*, and *Sandalwood*. His mood and writing are in sharp contrast to the realism of Sandburgian atmosphere. No idealization, in his woodland music, of the great machine of today, rather a turning away from industrialization and, as Max Nordau would say, the lies of civilization. He sings:
>
>> Let us leave the hateful town
>> With its stale, forgotten lies;
>> Far beneath renewing skies,
>> Where the piny slope goes down,
>> All with April love and laughter—
>> None to leer and none to frown—
>> We shall pass and follow after
>> Shattered lace of water spun
>> On a steep and stony loom
>> Down the paths of laurel-gloom.
>
> A disciple of Poe and Baudelaire, he has gone as far into the regions of the weird and terrible as either of the elder poets. For what is called "pure" poetry, one shall search for his equal in vain among contemporary poets.

As we can see from this quotation (these are the first ten lines of "Adventure," from *Sandalwood*)—and we could cite other examples by Smith or Nora herself—a very real affinity, a spiritual kinship, a certain shared idealization, exists between these two poets and their work, above all in their love of nature as exemplified in the Californian landscape, either of the south or of the north. In January 1911, then on the threshold of creating his first mature poetry, Smith began his correspondence with Sterling, an exchange with poems and related materials that would last the death of the older poet on 17 November 1926 at the Bohemian Club. Writing to Sterling on 24 March 1912 from Auburn, the young Smith asked after Nora May's one and only book. "I have no intention of taking Nora May French's method of escape. By the way, can you tell me who publishes her poems, and also the title and price of the volume? I intend to add it to my little collection of present-day poetry as soon as I can."

In his reply dated 10 April 1912 from Carmel, Sterling responds: "I'll send you one of Nora May's books soon. Don't bother to buy one." On 9 June 1912, after he has had almost two months to absorb the book, following receipt of it from his mentor, Smith acknowledges the gift in his letter to Sterling, and with a rare enthusiasm, at least for the rather atrabilious young poet.

> Many, many thanks to you for the lovely volume of Nora May French's poems. They're all wonderful, and some of them have stirred me more than anything I have seen, in many a day. I love them all . . . And that wonderful face! I think this little book should live, if the love of poetry survives the materialistic smother of the present age. And I'm glad it's so well gotten out, in this day of meretriciously bound and cheaply printed books. There's no discord between the cover and the contents.

In his letter dated 11 June 1912 from Carmel, Sterling in his own turn acknowledges with pleasure the enthusiasm that the book has aroused in his pupil and protégé: "I knew you'd like Nora May's poems. She wrote in crystal, and I'm sure the writing will endure. The book was well gotten up because we her friends published it. I've thirty of the books here in my cabin, which once she occupied."

During July 1912, while he sojourned as an honored guest at Sterling's place in Carmel, Smith learned much more about Nora directly from someone who had lived virtually next to her almost until she died. It was the young poet's first exposure to the pristine natural beauty of the Monterey peninsula, even then still mostly undeveloped, commingling as it does rocky coast, unparalleled ocean, forested hills and lowlands, grassy open spaces, and panoramic sky. Years later, in the memoir that he wrote around 1941, "George Sterling: Poet and Friend," Smith recalls this first and happiest sojourn in Carmel, particularly the elder poet's recollections of the increasingly legendary Nora May French. Smith's own remembrance thus records certain details of her last days and writing otherwise unknown and unchronicled:

> At the time of my visit, Sterling had given the use of his house to John Kenneth Turner, author of *Barbarous Mexico*, and Turner's wife and children, Turner being in temporary financial difficulties. Sterling was occupy-

ing the little cabin he had built for Nora May French; but, turning this over to me, he moved into a little tent for the duration of my stay.

He spoke often of Nora May French, that strange and tragically gifted girl who had ended her life with poison in the same bed in which I slept nightly. She had, it seems, previously attempted to shoot herself with his revolver and had brought him a tress of her ashen-blonde hair clipped away by the bullet. He showed me the very spot beside the path up the ravine where this attempt had occurred, according to her statement. But, oddly, there had been no powder marks on her hair. I do not recall that he attributed her suicide to unrequited love for James Hopper; but there had been other reasons . . . perhaps sufficient ones.

She was, he said, the most changeable person he had ever known: incredibly radiant and beautiful at times; at others, absolutely dull and colorless in her appearance. One day he brought out a manuscript of hers dictated during the delirium of illness. It was full of an otherworldly weirdness; but I can remember nothing of it, but that it was "such stuff as dreams are made of" and therefore immemorable as dreams.

On one occasion, I recall that George told me to keep the cabin door shut at night. "If you don't," he warned, "the cat will come in and jump on the bed. You'll think it's Miss X— trying to climb into bed with you, and you'll be scared." "Oh, no," I rejoined, "I'll probably think it's Nora May's ghost, and I won't be scared at all. I'm sure that her ghost would be a lovely one." "You certainly have an imagination," he commented, half admiringly, half deprecatingly.

(This memoir was first published in *Mirage*, Winter 1963–64. Either Smith makes a mistake about the bed in which he slept being the same one in which Nora died, or Sterling had moved that original bed from the main bedroom in the bungalow into the little cabin alongside the bungalow, sometime after Nora's decease.)

Although they could never have met in person, the special relationship that existed between Nora May French and Clark Ashton Smith by the unique means of George Sterling as their mutual friend and medium found expression not quite a decade later when Ashton Smith created his magnificent piece of homage in blank verse, "To Nora May French." In his letter of 10 July 1920, Smith reports to Sterling on his recently created poems. It is possible that his tribute to Nora May cost him rather more travail than some of his other poems did, and for that reason he may have felt less than enthusiastic about his achievement as embodied in this work.

> I liked all the poems that you sent me. [. . .] I wish I could send you something good in return; my blank verses on Nora May French appear tedious, rambling, uninspired. Pass them on to Lafler, if you care for them at all. Possibly they are not as bad as I think—I'm no competent or impartial judge of anything at present, since I feel disgusted with everything I have ever written.

As soon as possible, in his letter of 26 August 1920 from San Francisco, Sterling disabuses the younger poet of his poor opinion of his own work, and in no uncertain terms.

> You don't seem to care for your poem to Nora May French, but to me it seems a very lovely thing, and I'm sure Lafler will think the same of it as soon as I've shown it to him—a thing I've neglected to do so far.
> [. . .]
> Oh yes! The poem to Nora May is *solid poetry*. I wish I'd a signed copy to send to [Walter Adolphe] Roberts, late editor of "Ainslee's" [Magazine]. He is a Nora May enthusiast, and would greatly appreciate it.

Presumably Sterling did show or send a copy of this tribute to both Lafler and Roberts, and presumably they both enjoyed it and thought highly of it. Indeed, because of the enthusiasm that Roberts felt for Nora May and her poetry, a fine sonnet by Louise Gebhard Cann, "Nora May French, in Memoriam," had already made its appearance in *Ainslee's* for November 1919. Notwithstanding, Smith's piece of homage remains the best single tribute, as well as the most substantive, ever penned to her memory. Smith's identification of Nora May with the ocean in all its timeless beauty and variety of color, mood, and creature is nothing less than inspired—not to mention his further identification of the beautiful dead poet with mythical or legendary persons or things associated with the sea, such as Atlantis, Lemuria, Sappho, Mytilene, Lesbos, and so forth.

When he included this tribute in *Ebony and Crystal*, his third collection, published in December 1922, a full ten years after his first and happiest sojourn in Carmel, Smith appended this notice at the end of the almost 100-line poem, divided into two near-equal sections: "Nora May French, the most gifted poet of her sex that America has produced, died by her own hand at Carmel in 1907. Her ashes were strewn into the sea from Point Lobos."

As reported in Sterling's correspondence, as in his letter to Smith dated 27 July 1915 from San Francisco, Lafler as Nora May's erstwhile lover once planned a book of tributes both in verse and in prose dedicated to his own protégée's memory.

> Did you ever write anything about Nora May French? And if not, do you care to? Lafler thinks of getting out a book comprised of various prose and poetical "tributes" to her. Loveman says he's [working] on an elegy to her now. Lafler's beautiful "Pearl" was to her; and *I* have two or three things, as you know.

The book of tributes never materialized, and if Samuel Loveman ever completed his elegy, it has not surfaced. A fine lyric poet who resided most of his life in the northeast, Loveman (1887–1976) was yet another of the many writers and bookmen encouraged by Sterling, and one who became a friend to Smith, as well as a profound admirer of Smith's own work, initially through Sterling and then through correspondence independent of their mentor. Loveman introduced H. P. Lovecraft to Smith through letters during 1922 but before the publication of *Ebony and Crystal* late that year. Thus it happened that Nora May French, like Ambrose Bierce before him, emerged as one of the earliest of those California poets and writers who became personally the focus of legend, rumor, myth, and posthumous admiration thanks to other poets and writers who continued their tradition such as Lafler, Sterling, Loveman, and Smith.

Despite his excellent intentions, undoubtedly sincere, Lafler never made good on them—quite apart from "The Pearl," his undeniably fine tribute. Not only did he fail to publish the memorial volume that he planned in Nora May's honor; he also failed in his other excellent, and far more important, intention concerning the beautiful dead poet and her small but unique body of work. In a letter dated sometime in October 1919, Sterling informed W. Adolphe Roberts that Lafler had recently earned over $10,000 in real-estate commissions and planned to bring out a new printing or edition of Nora May's *Poems*. Lafler evidently planned the new printing for 1920, ten years after the original one. Roberts meanwhile published an article on Nora May and her poetry that had made its appearance by May 1920. Lafler never did go through with his evidently serious plans for another edition of Nora May's poetry.

Neither ten years after her book of poems first appeared, nor yet another ten years after that, had Lafler republished her little volume. Nor had he done so by 14 January 1935, when he died in a car crash near San Jose on his way back from Big Sur, fifty miles north of that same Carmel where Nora May had committed suicide twenty-seven years before. (Sterling died on 17 November 1926 in his room at the Bohemian Club in the Montgomery Building, or Monkey Block, in downtown San Francisco.) Lafler had undoubtedly played the pivotal role in Nora May's life as a young adult. His invitation for her to come up to Northern California from Los Angeles initiated the whole series of events that resulted in her death. Still, it was Nora May herself who chose to move north and to commit suicide.

(Born in Jamaica of mixed West Indian and Caribbean descent, Walter Adolphe Roberts (1886–1962) was not only an editor of some prominence, as, for example, of *Ainslee's* during the 1910s, but also a short story and article writer and a prolific poet and connoisseur of poetry. His active period as published writer and editor appears to be around 1906–26, and he contributed to a wide variety of magazines, including the *Overland Monthly*, *Outing*, the *Bookman*, the *Forum*, *Current Opinion*, *Century Magazine*, and the *Saturday Review of Literature* among other periodicals. *The Review of Reviews* published his "Portrait" in the issue for October 1919. Although his article on Nora May French has not yet surfaced since Sterling and Lafler's time, it is clearly worth seeking out and finding, but a search through the *Reader's Guide to Periodical Literature*, as well as through *Ainslee's*, for the late 1910s and early 1920s does not reveal anything, so that, wherever it may have appeared, the periodical in question, with offices possibly located on or near the American West Coast, was not indexed in the *Reader's Guide*.)

In 1936 the Book Club of California chose Nora May's poetry for the second booklet in their series of California poets and writers, thus "The California Literary Pamphlets." Containing eighteen of her best poems, this booklet, *Poems by Nora May French*, also featured a fine and sympathetic evaluation of Nora May's work in the form of a foreword by Sara Bard Field (1882–1974), another poet of the American West. This foreword remains to date one of the best things written so far about the beautiful dead poet and her idiosyncratic work. If Nora May had lived, as Sara Bard Field herself admits like others both before and since, "She might have taken her place among America's foremost women poets." Although much more limited in size and scope, this booklet served in one sense as a kind of substitute for the second edition of Nora May's poems that Lafler had failed to publish.

Sometime before 1933, and probably soon after *Poems* appeared in 1910, another female lyric poet who has remained well known and respected perused Nora's little volume and confessed herself both impressed and moved: Sara Teasdale (1884–1933), herself born but a few years after Nora May's own birth in 1881. According to Richard Hughey, "Teasdale and the poet Sara Bard Field [. . .] both agreed that had she lived she would have become one of the most important poets of the twentieth century."

Just as all admirers of Nora May's work owe Lafler a great debt of gratitude for preserving almost all of what we have of her poems, so do they also owe Judith Allen a similar debt of gratitude for her master's thesis, "The Life and Writing of Nora May French," produced for the English Department of Mills College, Oakland, in 1963, more than a quarter of a century after the Book Club of California booklet. This thesis, the product of her labor in the early 1960s, was compiled and composed mostly during 1963. To this opus Nora May's own sister Helen French Hunt contributed enormously. Indeed, without her help and information the thesis would probably not exist at all, and thus it remains to this day the only real source of information on Nora May's life and her poetry.

In deference to sister Helen's express wishes, Allen had to leave certain facts unrecorded or in obscurity, such as Nora's first love affair, the one with her handsome cousin in New York City, 1899–1900; the consummated love affair between Henry Anderson Lafler and herself, 1906–07; and one or more pregnancies. Otherwise, the thesis contains just about everything that we have concerning Nora May's life and creativity. However, compared to the other evaluations that we have so far presented or mentioned, Allen's appraisal of Nora May's poetry seems, though perfectly competent, rather unadventurous and understated. She seems to miss the unique or essential quality of Nora May's work in verse. We quote in full Allen's final paragraph embodying her summation of Nora May's poetic art.

> It would be misleading to indulge in elaborate praise of the poetry of Nora May French; one cannot fairly charge that it has been unjustly ignored. The young woman who wrote the verses and letters quoted in this paper was an interesting and complex person. She wrote a small amount of poetry worthwhile primarily because her sincerity and her love of poetry make her writing come alive. Like most beginning poets, particularly minor ones, she was traditional in form and imagery, and her discoveries about herself and her world are more touching than original. Her personal conflicts were those of many of the young women of her era; and she can occasionally express them in a line which is truly memorable. A study of her life and writing is principally valuable in showing in some detail the struggles of a young artist in the local scene two generations ago.

One might conceivably challenge much or even most of this careful but faint-hearted summary, but we shall content us with objecting only to the anachronism in one sentence. "Like most beginning poets, particularly minor ones, she was traditional in form and imagery. . . ." By the years of her poetic maturity, say 1905–07, Nora May had ceased to be a beginning poet (that phase had started in 1894 at the age of twelve), at a time when poetry in free verse or free form had not yet become the near universal practice that it has today, following the lead of Walt Whitman and his revolutionary collection *Leaves of Grass* (1855–92). The vast majority of poets, whether beginning or otherwise, continued to use or adapt the traditional prosody as it had evolved in English up to that time, and would in fact continue to do thus at least until the 1920s and the further experiments of T. S. Eliot and Ezra Pound.

Properly concerned with her own personal and poetic priorities, Nora May demonstrates in her own work that she clearly knows her own identity and that she can accomplish what she wants or intends to achieve, following in particular the lead of Tennyson and Housman, perfectly good or distinctive models. As to her status as poet, we have no intention of getting us lost in that endless and fruitless quagmire, the issue or non-issue of major versus minor poets, whether in history or in theory, beyond stating the obvious. Such a classification, at once too simplistic and restrictive, has never functioned in any manner as an adequate or ideal system of dealing with the whole phenomenon of poets and poetry in any language—unless we add a further and much needed category, thereby avoiding the whole futile non-issue of major and minor.

Major poets in the sense of Homer, Virgil, Dante, Chaucer, Spenser, Marlowe, Ronsard, Milton, Victor Hugo, and others—or to cite the rare lyric female poet such as Sappho, whose work all Graeco-Roman antiquity revered as much as that of Homer—have never existed in great abundance by the very nature of things. But many notable or significant poets with unique and personal voices have indeed existed in many languages throughout history. In such an expanded classification we would call Nora May French definitely a significant poet, perhaps more interesting and important than many of the better-known modernist poets coming after her. Beyond the fact that she did not live long enough to continue maturing as a poet— and hence could not fully live up to the potential that she evidently possessed—Nora May had nonetheless produced a small corpus of unique work of lasting value.

In his original note appended to his tribute to Nora May French as published in *Ebony and Crystal* (1922), we should notice exactly what Clark Ashton Smith says of her in an evaluative sense—"the most gifted poet of her sex that America has produced"—thus, not the greatest, but the most naturally gifted American female poet, as perceived up into the early 1920s. Because of her early death she could not exploit the full potential of her amazing poetic gift, which in time could very well have revealed itself as pure genius. Nevertheless, what Nora May French managed to accomplish before her death, however small in quantity, remains a solid and substantial achievement of singular character. One cannot realistically ask more than that of any poet whose work is worth reading, pondering, cherishing.

Although she belongs just as much to Southern California as to Northern California (after all she resided in the Los Angeles area from 1888 on into latter 1906), Nora May French has become in a larger sense almost forgotten in the California Southland except by Californian literary specialists and by the occasional and historically knowledgeable poetry-lover. However, her firm identification with the California Romantics, whose floruit occurred in the approximate period 1890 to 1930, has ensured for her in Northern California at least a somewhat larger and more enduring audience. Since 1963, whether located in, or speaking from or for, the northern or southern halves of the state, various individuals, some of them distinctive as well as distinguished, have not hesitated to pronounce and promulgate glowing and heartening endorsements of Nora May's unique poetic gifts. Here are several examples. In 1985 Oxford University Press published *Inventing the Dream*—that is, the California Dream—by Kevin Starr, a defining volume in the outstanding series by the same author on Californian history, politics, culture, and so forth. In section II, "Pasadena and the Arroyo," he has this to say concerning the Golden Girl:

> . . . [Charles] Lummis favored women writers [for his magazine *Out West*], and none more so than a hauntingly beautiful Occidental College undergraduate, Nora May French. A spirited horsewoman and lover of the sea, Nora May French wrote poems bristling with realized Southern California imagery—the sundown Pacific, the Arroyo itself, a mission garden, sagebrush, desert flowers—all of it put in service to a pervasive plaintiveness, a sadness she felt at the heart of things, as if she foresaw her own fate. Or was this sadness a self-fulfilling prophecy? After all, she would later claim that "all sensible people will ultimately be damned." In any event, she of the curly

hair and the soft eyes was dead from cyanide of potassium in the early hours of 14 November 1907 on George Sterling's porch in Carmel: done in by her vulnerability to Eros (a succession of affairs, a number of abortions), sick with confusion over having loved unwisely and not well. At the funeral services on Point Lobos a quarrel broke out among a number of men as to who would have the right to cast her ashes into the sea.

Following in the wake of the Book Club of California's booklet (1936), several other booklets with her poetry have appeared as published by notable admirers. We mention here the two such known to us, the first one *Nora May French: Her Poems*, brought out by Star Rover House in 1986, with an incisive and sympathetic introduction by poet and literary historian Mary Rudge and headed with a brief but vivid memorial by poet Dorothy Jesse Beagle. Released in Oakland at the Jack London Heritage House in an edition of 500 copies, this handsome softbound book of 70 pages contains 18 selections like the Book Club of California's pamphlet, duplicating not quite half the same poems. This timely reprinting of some of Nora May's poems reflects very well on all those involved.

The second booklet or pamphlet, issued by Richard Kohlman Hughey, appeared as recently as July 2003 and contains the entire sequence of "The Spanish Girl" followed by "The Garden of Dolores." In his brief but pithy foreword (dated "Pollock Pines, California / Thursday, July 3, 2003"), Hughey summarizes in a capable way the essential character of Nora May's poetry.

> Nora May . . . left behind a small treasury of poems of exquisite gemlike quality. Although she never matured psychologically, her poetry exhibited a mastery of the traditional verse of the times expressed simply and without the excessive diction and classical allusions of her contemporaries. Though written almost one hundred years ago, her verses still have a fresh, spring-like quality as though they were written yesterday. They are nature-loving, whimsical, and feminine; and they compare quality favorably with the best poetry of Sara Teasdale, Edna St. Vincent Millay, and, even, Emily Dickinson. Teasdale and the poet Sara Bard Field, in fact, read Nora May's collection of poems, and they both agreed that had she lived she would have become one of the most important poets of the twentieth century."

Also in 2003, Heyday Books, a California press, brought out a comprehensive anthology edited by Dana Gioia, Chryss Yos, and Jack Hicks, *Cali-*

fornia Poetry: From the Gold Rush to the Present. In presenting the selection of poems from Nora May's work, Dana Gioia gives us in a brief account one of the best extant summaries of Nora May's life and work and also pinpoints the unique appeal of that poetry. After years of mainstream neglect, Gioia's remarks on her poems constitute quite a welcome and noteworthy critical appreciation.

The poetry of Nora May French has already generated much comment and appreciation since its publication in magazines, newspapers, and the occasional collection, and will continue to do so. As established by the statement of her own sister in February 1963, no one in her family compiled a cache of her manuscripts, prose or poetry, in order to create an official archive of her work for safekeeping in some appropriate library. Without Lafler, Sterling, Garnett, and probably others, no cache of her poems after her death would have existed from which to compile the contents of her *Poems*. All the poems and other materials accompanying the extant letters of Nora May, George and Carrie Sterling, Henry Anderson Lafler, Jimmy Hopper, as well as some from Nora May to her sister Helen, as preserved in the Bancroft and Huntington libraries, represent almost the entirety of work by and about Nora May French, unless a cache of unpublished material exists in some undisclosed location.

Because the French family did not rate her early work very highly, any more than Nora May herself, and because Nora May like her family was apparently waiting for her poetry to gain strength and maturity before they or she would have brought out a book of her poems, no one could have anticipated that what we have of her work represents the material that happened to survive at the time of her death. Nora May left behind her a very small legacy of poems, fewer than one hundred. That is all of it, but it suffices. It represents not just her poetic promise, but also genuine poetic achievement. It is possible that in maturing both she and her poetry might have lost the very qualities that we most admire about it and hence about their author.

Like her technique, Nora May's poetry is admittedly simple, but neither simplistic nor simple-minded. Instead, it is the clear and compact simplicity (pregnant, if you will) that we have learned to associate with the classics, with classical poetry as exemplified in various languages, beginning with Greek and Latin, and continuing with such Romance tongues as Italian, French, Catalan, Spanish, and Portuguese, together with German and English. Only Judith Allen and Sara Bard Field have complained, and then only mildly, about what they consider the principal defect of her poetry, a certain rhythmic monotony.

According to Judith Allen, "Both her life and her work bear the mark of the California romanticism of the turn of the century" [i.e., 1899–1901], "the somewhat monotonous rhythm of much of her poetry." Allen aligns this with the "highly romantic" character of George Sterling's own poems, categorized as "regular metrical compositions—often lyrical, more often monotonous." Sara Bard Field states, "Her measure, inclining to monotony, might have acquired a various tone, a more subtle rhythm, a profounder sweep." To some extent this complaint seems valid, but it also serves as a reminder that many modern poets and modern critics, in repudiating the older prosodic traditions, do not themselves know how to sound, to read aloud, metrically precise poems.

The art of recital, of recitation, is exactly that, and requires practice and study—just as the art of declaiming and acting, especially in classical plays (like those of Shakespeare), demands the same by directors and actors—in order to reveal itself as the art that it remains. Recited or spoken aloud with nuance, emotion, and subtlety, the poetry of Nora May French comes amazingly to life, and only then reveals its full freshness, its full emotional treasures, and its often utter poignancy. The evidence that we possess in the letters by others during her lifetime indicates that she herself functioned as an effective and confident reader in public or in private. Even the "barbaric yawp" of Walt Whitman in his endless rhapsodical catalogues, no less than the rugged and seemingly unfettered rhythms of Robinson Jeffers, need care and study to make their full efficacy palpable when read aloud.

Those poets and critics who use and understand metrical precision and regularity have never complained about the monotonous rhythm of Nora May's poetical art—not Lafler, nor Sterling, nor Clark Ashton Smith, among many other literary figures. A more genuine mode or measure of the true stature peculiar to Nora May French is found in the tributes and other memorial poems created by fellow poets in her honor. Only there does the best and most lucid appreciation of herself and her poetic art make itself understood and profoundly felt.

Indeed, perhaps we can most readily define the special essence that constitutes her own unique appeal vis-à-vis the two leading male poets of the California Romantics, Sterling and Smith, whom poet and critic Witter Bynner, early on in his own career, once wittily termed the Star Dust Twins (in an interview conducted by Edward F. O'Day and published in *Town Talk* for 7 September 1912). The Star Dust Twins! Bynner created this playful nickname in imitation of the once well-known brand name of the powdered soap called the Gold Dust Twins. Thus the term, perhaps not so disrespectful or inaccurate as it might first appear, seems on second thought all the more suitable in the Age of Space today, given the cosmic-astronomic-mindedness that pervades the poetry of Sterling and Smith so powerfully and obsessively.

Whereas Smith and Sterling manifest their cosmic consciousness through the *macro*cosmic, that is, through a vast and extroverted "system" of emphatic cosmic-astronomic-mindedness, Nora May French demonstrates her own such consciousness through a quieter and more intimate perception of the *micro*cosmic. However, subtle touches of the macrocosmic betray themselves here and there in her poetry. The final stanza of "The Mission Graves" (conceived at a time long before anyone had a thought of restoring the California missions, most of which had fallen into ruin by 1900) features the souls of the dead returning from the cosmic dark to keep vigil for one lonely night: "Ah, the Dead knew! / The grateful Dead, far-called from voids of space." Again, as in the final stanza of "The Mourner," it is the night skies, with their immensitude of stars (as in the *oeuvre* of Sterling and Smith), that awaken Nora May's macrocosmic sensibility: "I am become beloved of the night— / Her huge sea-lands ineffable and far."

Characteristically, however, it is the microcosmic that claims this poet's attention and compassion, no less than our own, at first almost always off-guard in an emotional sense, as in the ineffably poignant "Best-Loved" or "Vivisection" or "By the Hospital." These pack a quiet but undeniable wallop. But no matter what the subject or the mood, Nora May knows instinctively how to spring an astute surprise that can take us unawares, even in the least significant-seeming piece. She can quickly transform what might appear at first as no more than a conventional but not unattractive word-picture into something deeper, darker, and potentially more riveting.

Take a seemingly innocuous example from among the fewer than a dozen "new" (or hitherto uncollected) pieces that we have discovered and added to the contents of the original book of poems published in 1910 ("My Maid of Dreams," "The Lost Chimneys," "The Panther Woman," "Poppies," "Answered," "Be Silent, Love," "How Ends the Day?," "A Dream-Love," "The Suicide," and "At the End"). This example is our first addition, "My Maid of Dreams," and follows "Oh, Dryad Thoughts." Only after perusing the poem in question and examining the details do we realize that the maiden of Nora May's particular or idiosyncratic dreams is none other than that goddess of seasonal change, and the queen of the infernal regions or of the realms of death and night, Persephone, the same awesome divinity celebrated by Swinburne in his "Hymn to Proserpine" or, more aptly, "The Garden of Proserpine."

Even more characteristically, perhaps, Nora May's quintessential quality reveals itself in the course of a given piece, where a single unexpected line suddenly opens up the poem and our consciousness into larger and unrestricted vistas and implications. When she takes a figurative drink from some twilight pool, as described in that souvenir from the summer of 1906, "In Camp," she sips "a tiny, shattered star, / Deep drinking from that mirrored sky." In "Yesterday" (one of her two last poems, the other being "The Mourner"), she again opens the final stanza in a quietly startling manner: "Above the world as twilight fell / I made my heart into a sky, / And through a twilight like a shell / I saw the shining sea-gulls fly." It is in lines like these that we hear the authentic voice of Nora May French: a still small voice that speaks to us from somewhere out of time and space—a still small voice that reminds us of our vulnerability amid the impassible vastitudes of the cosmos. The sense of enduring beauty that eluded her personally during her life, she yet succeeded in capturing through her posthumously published poems, as reprinted here almost one hundred years after her death.

—DONALD SIDNEY-FRYER,

Westchester, Los Angeles, California
14 November 2006.

Sources

The preceding account of the life and *oeuvre* of Nora May French, especially her life and its immediate aftermath, closely follows or parallels the text of "The Life and Writing of Nora May French," the M.A. thesis done by Judith Allen for the English Department of Mills College, Oakland, in 1963—except where corrected by the article "The King of Telegraph Hill," by Joanne Lafler, published in the *Argonaut: Journal of the San Francisco Museum and Historical Society*, Summer 2004, including issues not mentioned, or scarcely so, by Judith Allen out of deference to the wishes of Helen French Hunt, that the thesis-writer not emphasize her sister Nora May's love life.

In closely following Judith Allen's text, the author of the preceding account has also included several of her citations from letters written by James Marie Hopper and Carolyn Rand Sterling. However, the author has added several citations of his own from letters written by George Sterling to Ambrose Bierce, as well as half a dozen citations from the correspondence between Sterling and Clark Ashton Smith, 1911–26.

The corrections from Dr. Lafler's article involve the following topics relating to Henry Anderson Lafler and Nora May French: (1.) Lafler and French first met in person in Los Angeles in January 1906, not in late 1905. (2.) This was when they first made love; Nora become pregnant and had an abortion. (3.) Extant letters exchanged between Lafler and French cease to exist following the summer of 1906. (4.) Lafler took French to Carmel for the first time in August 1906 (not in August 1907), when she first met the Sterlings. (5.) Obtaining the use of a large lot on Telegraph Hill in San Francisco from the realtor Frank C. Havens, Lafler began building a number of bungalows on the land in 1906, but no evidence exists that the French sisters ever lived there. (6.) Both Lafler and Hiley were still married to their respective wives in the summer and fall of 1907, contrary to the statement by Judith Allen, and although he filed for divorce (from his first wife Alice Sherrill) in August 1907, Lafler did not pursue the matter until sometime later (once French reacted negatively to Lafler's evidently serious intention to marry her as soon as he was free), the divorce becoming final in 1910. (7.) French terminated her relationship with Lafler in August 1907, and the French sisters left San Francisco at the end of that month, Helen returning to Los Angeles before her sister would have done so, and Nora lingering in Carmel with the Sterlings.

At the present time Dr. Lafler is expanding her article into a full biography of Henry Anderson Lafler, and her colleague Pamela Herr is preparing a full biography of Nora May French. Both monographs will feature corrected and updated accounts of Nora May French's life, but in Dr. Lafler's case only insofar as Nora May's life impinged on that of Henry Anderson Lafler.

The Outer Gate

The Collected Poems of Nora May French

The Outer Gate

Life said: "My house is thine with all its store;
    Behold, I open shining ways to thee—
    Of every inner portal make thee free:
O child, I may not bar the outer door.
Go from me if thou wilt, to come no more;
    But all thy pain is mine, thy flesh of me;
    And must I hear thee, faint and woefully,
Call on me from the darkness and implore?"

Nay, mother, for I follow at thy will.
    But oftentimes thy voice is sharp to hear,
        Thy trailing fragrance heavy on the breath;
Always the outer hall is very still,
    And on my face a pleasant wind and clear
        Blows straitly from the narrow gate of Death.

Rain

The rain was grey before it fell,
    And through a world where light had died
There ran a mournful little wind
    That shook the trees and cried.

The rain was brown upon the earth,
    In turbid stream and tiny seas—
In swift and slender shafts that beat
    The flowers to their knees.

The rain is mirror to the sky,
    To leaning grass in image clear,
And drifting in the shining pools
    The clouds are white and near.

Best-Loved

It was a joy whose stem I did not break—
    A little thing I passed with crowded hands,
And gave a backward look for beauty's sake.

Of all I pulled and wove and flung aside,
    Was any hue preferred above the rest?
I only know they pleased me well, and died.

But this—it lives distinct in Memory's sight,
    A little thing, incurving like a pearl.
I think its heart had never seen the light.

THE ROSE

Ay, pluck a jonquil when the May's a-wing!
  Or please you with a rose upon the breast,
  A sweeter violet chosen from the rest,
To match your mood with blue caprice of spring—
Leave windy vines a tendril less to swing.
  Why, what's a flower? A day's delight at best,
  A perfume loved, a faded petal pressed,
A whimsey for an hour's remembering.

But wondrous careful must he draw the rose
  From jealous earth, who seeks to set anew
    Deep root, young leafage, with a gardener's art—
To plant her queen of all his garden close,
  And make his varying fancy wind and dew,
    Cloud, rain, and sunshine for one woman's heart.

Between Two Rains

It is a silver space between two rains;
    The lulling storm has given to the day
    An hour of windless air and riven grey;
The world is drained of color; light remains.
Beyond the curving shore a gull complains;
    Unceasing, on the bastions of the bay,
    With gleam of shields and veer of vaporing spray
The long seas fall, the grey tide wars and wanes.

It is a silver space between two rains:
    A mood too sweet for tears, for joy too pale—
    What stress has swept or nears us, thou and I?
This hour a mist of light is on the plains,
    And seaward fares again with litten sail
    Our laden ship of dreams adown the sky.

The Message

So might it brush my cheek with errant wings,
    So might it speak with thrilling touch and light
Of answering eyes, of dim, unuttered things—
    A moth from hidden gardens of the night.

So, in a land of hills, where twilight lay,
    Might come a sudden bird-call to the ear,
Across the canyons, faint and far away . . .
    O Heart, how sweet . . . half heard and wholly dear.

By the Hospital

Who goes to meet the windy night
    With unseen comrades shouting by,
Who grips a bough in swift delight
    To let it dip and loose and fly;

Who runs for rest that running gives,
    Runs till his throbbing muscles speak;
Who bends to feel how keenly lives
    The joyous grass beneath his cheek—

With sudden tears his eyes shall fill,
    With quick-drawn breath he sees them plain—
Those bodies that must lie so still,
    So tired—in the House of Pain.

"Oh, Dryad Thoughts"

Oh, Dryad thoughts of lovely yesterday! —
    You melted through a sunny wood like mist,
With here a wind of laughter, there a stray
    Pleased flower, tipped and kissed.

To-day among the noises of the street,
    The press of faces, sullen, gay, and wise,
I hear you calling, calling me; I meet
    Your clear, untroubled eyes.

My Maid of Dreams

Now foliaged darkness of low hills is kissed
With threaded pearl slim-white as maiden's wrist;
Now with the opal films of earliest mist
My Maid of Dreams comes to me . . . Milky fair,
Her face of changeful lights that shame the morn,
And twin blue hyacinths in her eyes are born,
Dawn glimmers phosphor-pale upon her hair.

Her face floats up to me thro' waters dark,
Beneath the wrinkled clearness whitely seen;
And filtering shafts of yellow noontide mark
Her gleaming fingers, glimpsed in flickering green.

The air grows jewel-red in widening spheres
From day's deep heart low burning in the West.
Sweet airs, blow cool the breath of earth's first tears—
Blow me my Maid of Dreams . . . Ah, dearest best!
Flame-lit thou comest thro' the silent land,
My poppy-crowned, dusk-eyed with visioned night!
Lead me, oh maid, with touch of guiding hand,
To lands unknown . . . to realms of new delight.

Music in the Pavilion

Faces that throng—and stare and come and go—
    The air a-quiver as the voices meet;
And loud Humanity in mingled flow
    Passes with jarring tread of many feet.

But over all the chatter of the crowd
    (The background for its delicate relief)
Now trembling in a thread, now wild and loud,
    The violin laughs and sings, and cries its grief.

Then, through it all, and round it all, the sea;
    A solemn heart with never-ceasing beat,
Bearing an undertone of mystery
    The harsh and lovely notes, the shrill and sweet.

Surely it is my life—of plodding days,
    With one Ideal holding clear and good;
And sounding over, under, through my ways,
    Something apart—and never understood.

Rebuke

The tortured river-banks, the toiling piers—
    I walked thereby as older grew the day,
And sick with sorry clamor in mine ears,
    Heart-weary turned my steps and went my way.

"O place full-voiced of wretchedness!" I cried.
    (The sun had set, the dusk was closing in)
O place where laboring Life goes heavy-eyed,
    Compound of grime and discord, strife and sin!"

I turned me back, and lo, a miracle!
    For misty violet lay along the land.
The shining river in mysterious spell
    (Divinely touched by some transmuting hand)

A path of wonder was, and on it stirred,
    (Black-shaped, and jeweled with a crimson spark)
A ship that slowly moved; and, faintly heard,
    A cheery song rose blithely to the dark.

In Camp

I

As down I bent with eager lips
    Above the stones and cresses cool—
The yellow tent, the little moon,
    I found within my twilight pool.

The fringing trees, the floating moon,
    The bubble tent—I passed them by,
And sipped a tiny, shattered star,
    Deep drinking from that mirrored sky.

II

My tent is shadowed day and night
    With leaves that shift in moon and sun;
Across its walls of lucent white
    The lovely varied tracings run;

And black and slender, quickly sped,
    I watch the little feet at dawn—
A sudden oriole overhead,
    A darting linnet come and gone.

The Nymph

From forest paths we turned us, nymphs, new-made,
      And, lifting eyes abashed with great desire
Before high Jove, the gift of souls we prayed.

Whereat he said: "O perfect as new leaves
      New glossed and veined with blood of perfect days
And stirred to murmured speech in fragrant eves,

"Still ask ye souls? Behold, I give instead
      Into each breast a bird with fettered wings,
A bird fast holden with a silken thread:

"To fall from trial of flight with strength swift spent,
      To sing of mating and the brooding grass,
To turn thy being earthward to content."

Within me sudden wrath and terror strove,
      And, casting forth his gift I cried aloud:
"I pray thee for a soul in truth, great Jove!"

Then smiled he slowly, lifting to my look
      A fabric where the rippled lustre played
And shifted like the humor of a brook—

All prism-hued, as upward eyes may see
      The sun through dazzled lashes. Straight I cried:
"I know not this!" "Thy soul," he answered me.

But when my joy had seized it, "Nay," he said,
      And cast it gleaming to the scattering wind—
Hues green and golden, blue and fervent red.

Within his hand the brightest shred of all—
      The very heart and secret of the web—
That held he fast and loosed he not at all;

But to me said: "O thou who scorned the dole
      That gave thee peace of days and long content,
Do now *my* will. Go forth and find thy soul."

To earth we went, nor knew I from that hour
      My sister's joy or pain; but on great morns
When low light slept above a world in flower,

Through drowsing noons where heat and color lie
      In ever wavering tides of airy seas,
Winged by the darting ships of dragon-flies—

Through these and twilight peace I went, and rid
      My steps of comrades. Lonely must I find
The silent places where my soul was hid.

In sheltered ways with summer showers sweet
      I wandered on a day, and singing found
The very green I sought beneath my feet.

In leafing forests when the year was new,
      And heaven ribboned in the crossing boughs,
I gathered marvelous strip on strip of blue.

When on a lonely stream the moon was bright,
      A Naiad from her treasure plucked me forth
Such gold as bound my web with threads of light.

And red. Ah, love! thou knowest how I came
      Unto thy fluting in the breathless eve,
And burned my heart's pale flower to scarlet flame! . . .

One morn I found within a drop of dew
      My very soul: a crystal world it was
Wherein the varied earth and heaven's blue

And myself gazing glassed in perfect sphere—
      But long above it was my wonder bent,
And lo! it dried more swiftly than a tear.

Now is this truth, O Jove, that I have won
      And woven all the shreds thou gav'st the wind?
But how, I pray thee, can my task be done

Unless thou ope thine hand, unless thou loose
      The very heart and secret of the web
Where every thread may end and know its use?

Joy hast thou not withheld, nor love denied,
      Nor any beauty dimmed on earth or sky;
Yet by thy will I roam unsatisfied.

But couldst thou hear again that earliest plea,
      Again my choice would flout the lesser gift,
And willing take this task thou grantest me—

To search the heart and secret of the whole,
    To twine the eager hues of varied days,
And to its bright perfection weave a soul.

VIVISECTION

We saw unpitying skill
    In curious hands put living flesh apart,
    Till, bare and terrible, the tiny heart
Pulsed, and was still.

We saw Grief's sudden knife
    Strip through the pleasant flesh of soul-disguise—
    Lay for a second's space before our eyes
A naked life.

The Stranger

She sat so quiet day by day,
    The sweet withdrawal of a nun,
With busy hands and downward eyes—
    The shyest thing beneath the sun.

Nor knew we, tossing each to each
    Our rapid speech, our careless words,
That through them, always, half-afraid,
    Her thoughts had gone like seeking birds,

Plucking a twig, a shining straw,
    A happy thread with silken gleams,
To carry homeward to her heart,
    And weave a hidden nest of dreams.

The Constant Ones

The tossing trees had every flag unfurled
    To hail their chief, but now the sun is set,
And in the sweet new quiet on the world
    The king is dead, the fickle leaves forget.

A placid earth, an air serene and still;
    In misty blue the gradual smoke is thinned—
Only the grasses, leaning to his will,
    The grasses hold a memory of wind.

INSTINCT

To Reason with the praise of one I go
To fall back, silent, at her whispered "No."

And always of the other says she, "Trust—
He doeth thus and thus, O thou unjust!"

Yet meet one eye to eye and queries end—
An eager hand goes out to greet a friend,

And let the other please me, soon or late
Wakes with a hiss the little snake of hate.

The Lost Chimneys

[San Francisco, Christmas, 1906.]

A jagged crown they topped the town,
    They stood in wind and weather—
Stout chimneys Santa clambered down
    For years and years together.
In all the havoc April wrought
    No shattered flue will hold him;
Who's given the good old Saint a thought—
    Has anybody told him?

He doesn't read as others do
    The daily publications;
He doesn't hear the whole year through,
    The gossip of the nations.
His skillful fingers, busy Saint,
    Make hobby-horses sleeker,
Daub all the Noah's arks with paint
    And give each lamb a squeaker.

He'll come with dolls for Lil and Sue,
    A train for little brother,
And find of house and hearth and flue
    No brick upon another!
Turn over in your Christmas dream
    And snore in guilty slumber
While Santa tires his bronco team
    To find your change of number!

San Francisco, New Year's, 1907

Said the Old Year to the New: "They will never welcome you
    As they sang me in and rang me in upon my birthday night—
All above the surging crowd, bells and voices calling loud—
    A throng attuned to laughter and a city all alight.

"Kind had been the years of old, drowsy-lidded, zoned with gold;
    They swept their purples down the bay and sped the homeward keel;
The years of fruits and peace, smiling days and rich increase—
    Too indolent with wine and sun to grasp the slaying steel.

"As my brothers so I came, panther-treading, silken, tame;
    The sword was light within my hand, I kept it sheathed and still—
The jeweled city prayed me and the laughing voices stayed me—
    A little while I pleased them well and gave them all their will.

"As a panther strikes to slay, so I wrenched my shuddering prey.
    I lit above the panic throng my torches' crimson flare;
For they made my coming bright and I gave them light for light—
    I filled the night with flaming wings and Terror's streaming hair.

"They were stately walls and high—as I felled them so they lie—
    Lie like bodies torn and broken, lie like faces seamed with scars;
Here where Beauty dwelt and Pride, ere my torches flamed and died,
    The empty arches break the night to frame the tranquil stars.

"Though of all my brothers scorned, I, betrayer, go unmourned,
    It is I who tower shoulder-high above the level years;
You who come to build anew, joy will live again with you,
    But mightiest I who walked with Death and taught the sting of tears!"

The Panther Woman

I face the tranquil day with tranquil eyes—
On high sea-hills my cheeks are cold with mist.
In white foam-fingers quick desire dies.

Dies as a strangled bird the wave has torn—
Ay, drowns and dies this winged desire of mine
In white sea-fingers of the tidal morn.

But I would kill the restless silken night,
And I would still the wings that beat the dark,
And grasp the little throat of heart's-delight,

And drown the savage will that understands
How love would laugh to clasp your bending head,
How love would hold your face in her two hands,

How love would press your angry lips apart,
And leave the willful bruising of her kiss
In the sweet satin flesh above your heart.

The Poppy Field

Beyond the tangled poppies lies a lake;
    And ever sings to him who muses here
    The murmur of the hidden streams and clear
That flow thereto by arching fern and brake.
But never, slumber-heavy, does he wake
    To heed the music calling in his ear,
    Nor ever knows the water, deep and near,
Ashine with silver lilies for his sake.

And never he will heed, that love of thine;
    The poppies of thy beauty drug his sleep;
    Nor heedest thou that I must hear the streams,
And follow all thy crystal thought and fine,
    And love at last the lilies folded deep
    Within thy soul's unknown beyond his dreams.

Poppies

Where saffron poppy-petals curl apart,
Deep glowing lies the warmth of summer's heart.

Touch but a poppy-petal, satin-sleek,
And know the living silk of summer's cheek.

This curving blossom cup beneath her gaze
Brims with the filtered gold of perfect days;

Then o'er the hills she smiles—and one by one,
Lo! poppies quiver yellow to the sun.

You

All elfish woodland things that Fancy broods—
The comrades of my solitary moods—
Would crouch when heavy footsteps passed them by,
And peer from shelter—freakish folk and shy.

At you they pricked their furry ears in doubt;
Then, "This one sees—he knows!" they cried, "Come out!"
They thought to hush their piping till you passed.
"Come out!" they cried. "We dare be brave at last!"

So forth the gay procession sways and weaves;
And some are crowned with roses, some with leaves,
And all are mine, but some I never knew.
I could not wake them, but they come for you.

Just a Dog

So many times in those dark days,
    Instinct with sudden hope he crept,
(When sad, infrequent hands would raise
    The startled notes where sound had slept)
Seeking the voice he used to hear,
    Close-crouching at his master's knees,
Hoping to find again the dear
    Familiar hand upon the keys.

In very truth there was a soul
    Behind his brown and faithful eyes.
There live some mortals, on the whole
    Less loving, tender, loyal, wise;
And though we give it to decay,
    His poor old body, worn and scarred;
Yet He who judges soul and clay
    Will give one dog his just reward.

And that would be to let him come
    Toward dim-heard music, far and sweet;
Seeking with eyes rejoiced and dumb;
    Seeking with swift, unerring feet,
With love supreme to guide him true,
    Across the misty ways of space,—
Until he found the one he knew,
    And looked into his master's face.

Mirage

I see upon the desert's yellow rim,
    Beyond the trodden sand and herbage white
    Of level noon intolerably bright,
A purple lure of love divine and dim.
I hasten toward the fronded palm trees slim—
    The fountains of the city of delight—
    And stand bewildered to my heart's despite
In empty plains where hot horizons swim.

Will I who love the vision gain at last
    For very love of love the city's gates?
        I, weary, desert-wandering, knowing this:
That waiting me the golden doors are fast,
    And fathom-deep in dream the Princess waits,
        Her curving mouth uplifted for the kiss.

Dusk

Earth's parchèd lips
    Drink coolness once again, for daylight dies.
The young moon dips,
    A threaded gleam where sunset languid lies,
    And slowly twilight opens starry eyes.

Low in the West
    Day's fading embers cast a last faint glow
Behind a crest
    Where curving hills on primrose paleness show
    Sharp-lined in jet. Dusk stillness broods below.

A first long sigh
    Stirs from the broad and dew-wet breast of night.
The leaves reply
    With soft small rustling, moths take ghostly flight,
    And waking crickets shrill long-drawn delight.

The Spanish Girl

PART I

I. The Vine

To screen this depth of shade that sleeps
    Beyond the garden's shine,
On José's careful strings there creeps
    A little slender vine.

José is kind . . . but age is cold:
    My laughter meets his sigh.
The house is old, the garden old—
    Oh, young, the vine and I!

I love the web of light it weaves
    Across my half-drawn thread;
It's speech to me of waking leaves,
    While José hears his Dead.

So, ever reaching, tendril-fine,
    My eager visions run;
So, as the long day passes, twine
    My thoughts, shot through with sun.

II. The Chapel

The vanished women of my race,
    The daughters of a moldering year,
Set often in this quiet place
    Their votive tapers burning clear.

The patient waxen wreaths they wove,
    They hung before the Virgin's shrine;
To them it was a work of love,
    José decrees it task of mine!

They glimmer where a portrait swings—
    Women as proud and white as death—
Ah, they could mold those lifeless things;
    They had no blood, they had no breath.

"For holiness and meekness strive"
    (José would have me pray their prayers).
Now, Mary, warm and all alive,
    You shall not think me child of theirs.

So many waxen prayers you heard!
    If I should heap your altar high
With boughs that knew the nesting bird,
    With flowers that bloomed against the sky,

And let my wondering soul ascend
    In vivid question, swift surmise—
I think your shadowy face would bend,
    And look at me with startled eyes.

III. The Garden

They planted lilies where they might,
    A drift of Vestals slim and tall,
That lined these winding paths with white,
    That filled the court from wall to wall.

They shrank from savage, splendid heat,
    As from their teasing fires of Hell—
Only when morns and eves were sweet
    They walked and liked their garden well.

Slow moving through a pallid mist,
    Always in black, in black they came,
With busy rosary on wrist . . .
    And all the summer world aflame!

I planted flowers that know the sun,
    I brought them in from field and stream,
I passed not by the smallest one
    That pleased me with a yellow gleam;

Then in a hidden chest I found
    The marvel of an old brocade—
Strange figures on an azure ground,
    With threads of crimson overlaid,

And when the noon is fierce and bright,
    Along the garden, fold on fold,
My silken splendor like a light
    I trail between the aisles of gold.

IV

Across José's unending drone
    (Some ancient tale of arms and doom)
There came a poignant sweetness blown
    From sleeping leagues of orange bloom.

And lo! the steady candles blurred
    Like shining fishes in a net,
And José's kindly voice I heard—
    "But little one, thine eyes are wet."

He vowed the tale had made me weep,
    Its shadowy woes in courtly speech,
Nor knew they passed like wraiths of sleep
    The heart a vagrant wind could reach.

How can I tell, whose fancy floats
    As swift and passionate impulse veers,
What gust may sweep its roseleaf boats
    Adown a sudden tide of tears?

V

Where man has marred and nature yields,
    And never plant nor beast is free,
Along the tame and trampled fields
    An old unrest has followed me.

Now walk alone the night and I
    On foaming reaches curving stark,
And battling with a windy sky
    The stormy moon is bright and dark.

Facing the sea with streaming hair,
    My broken singing flung behind,
Whipped by the keen exultant air
    Till lips must close and eyes are blind,

Loving the sharp and cruel spray,
    The great waves thundering, might on might,
The pagan heart must shout and sway,
    Tossed in the passion of the night.

VI

Oh, never wings the Sisters chide,
    Wild upward wings that shine and blur,
Nor mourn they winds of eventide
    That bid the rhythmic garden stir,

And yet this life I cannot still,
    This winged and restless strength of flight,
That swings me down a singing hill
    Or answers to the calling night,

They curb when I would dance, would dance!
    By all the graven Saints, it seems
Most strange they make for my mischance
    No grim confessional of dreams!

The flower of Heart's Desire is sown
    In fields unknown to waking sight,
Down glittering spaces, all alone
    I whirl the fire of my delight—

Then, on the music's ebb and flow,
    Pause as a poising bird is hung,
With supple body swaying slow,
    With parted lips and arms up-flung.

VII

Always of Heaven the Sisters tell,
    Although of earth I question most—
I would I knew the world as well
    As Peter and the Angel host!

José may journey, never I.
    In all the lonely hours I spend.
He bids me tell my beads and sigh. . . .
    I wonder if the Saints attend?

For when the moon is small and thin
    And night is fragrant on the land.
The earth and I are so akin
    I think no Saint could understand.

Something within me sleeps by day;
    To moon and wind its petals part. . . .
It is not for my soul I pray;
    Ah Virgin!—for my untried heart.

PART II

I

This weak and silken love that meshes me
    Break strand from strand, O branches of the hill!
Brave wind that whips me breathless, tear me free!
    The witch's cobweb clings and shivers still.

Now ferns there were, and fretted sun above:
    I plunged me where the silver water fell,
But could not drown the little singing love—
    The little love that murmured like a shell.

Swift, swift, to drink my freedom at its flood,
    I ran with flying feet and lips apart,
But love was wilder than my leaping blood—
    Ah, louder than the beating of my heart.

II

I must not yield . . . but if he would not sing!
    My stilling hands upon my breast can feel
Its answer tremble like a muted string.
    Below the vaulted window where I kneel

He sings, he sings, to stars and listening skies.
    A white and haunted place my garden seems.—
I see the pleading beauty of his eyes
    As faces glimmer in a pool of dreams.

So wooing wind might sweep a harp awake.
    (Oh, muting fingers on each quivering string!)
I must not yield . . . I think my heart will break.
    Mother of Heaven, if he would not sing!

III

Now bending like a windy stem I strive,
    Yet ever onward, step by step, descend.
The silence is a threat, the dark alive,
    And love how far, how far, my journey's end.

It is the girlhood dream I leave behind,
    And sweeter vision never witched a maid.
Into the threatening shades I wander blind:
    Ah, Mary, help me now! I am afraid.

Yet with my fears I sway and follow still;
    The doorway gleams, the pleading magic charms,
Step after step, with fluttering breath and will—
    Step after step . . . at last . . . into his arms.

IV

Beyond this purple shadow glows
    My golden garden loud with bees,
And windy grey and silver flows
    Along the slopes of olive trees.

Before a sleeping flower uncurled,
    Before the early winds were born,
I woke for joy in such a world,
    And with the linnets shared the morn.

Remembering love, I woke and smiled,
    And heard the morning linnets sing,
And sang for love, and they for wild
    Delight of song and sun and spring.

V

Surely a brightness moves with me,
    For José gazes long and sighs,
Above the pages dim to see
    For ghosts of youth that brush his eyes.

And gazing long, old Marta said:
    "Some new device has made thee fair,
Yet have I often seen these red
    Pomegranate flowers against thy hair."

I would not have them understand
    The hidden thoughts that give me grace,
Nor guess the lights that dreams have fanned,
    And read their shining in my face.

But all my heart the Virgin knows.
    Before her eyes, so wise they were,
I laid my secret like a rose:
    "Mother, I love!" I cried to her.

VI

I had no more imagined love
    Than dreams the moonflower of its blue.
What sun that warmed its shielding glove,—
    What long blind eve that gave it dew,

Could tell that hueless folded thing
    Of shining texture silken-loomed,
Or say what marveling birds would sing
    The morning that it thrilled and bloomed?

Always it knew in groping thought
    Some end would come, some bloom must be,
The blind fulfilment that it wrought
    Was strained from darkness restlessly;

Till exquisite completion willed
    The answered bud, the dream put by,
And left the flower all sunned, and stilled
    With sudden wonder of the sky.

VII

My eyes are level with the grass,
      And up and down each slender steep
I watch its tiny people pass.
      The sun has lulled me half asleep.

And all beneath my breath I sing . . .
      This joy of mine is sweet to hold!
Such treasure had the miser king
      Who brushed the very dew to gold.

Deep in the sunny grass I lie
      And breathe the garden scents wind-driven,
So happy that if I should die
      They could not comfort me with Heaven.

PART III

I

One time I felt the sun in all my veins,
      And bloomed on crystal mornings, flower-wise,
And mourned as roses sadden in long rains.
      What pain is this the summer noon denies?

One time the hands of wind upon my hair
      Could heal me like a mother's touch and kiss.
When I could give my airy griefs to air
      I never knew so sharp a thorn as this.

The joy of flower and wind and sighing bough—
      It comes not back again for tears and rue.
A year agone I had not sought as now,
      And found the sky a vault of empty blue.

II

He loves no more. Upon the failing streams
      The summer burns—so burns another flame:
I see his eyes alight with alien dreams . . .
      That long-forgotten country whence he came

Calls to him past my words; beyond my eyes
      Lost waters shine, remembered sunsets die.
Ay, in my kiss another mouth replies,
      And speaks of kisses past, of lips put by.

Now this my heart divines, for words of love
      He gives me still (O woeful heart and bruised
To still complain!) . . . . But surely, when I move
      His eyes will never follow as they used.

III

The soul that made love exquisite is gone,
    It is not that the word, the kiss, is changed.
I cannot say, "Here was his thought withdrawn;
    So once was love, so now is love estranged."

But all of love that I could touch and know
    I held as one a lamp that makes his day,
And touch it still, and see its flame burn low,
    Its shining figures fade to painted clay.

Ah, I would hold the semblance, keep the kiss;
    But watching in its heart the paling spark,
I cry out when the shadows menace this,
    As children weep for terror of the dark.

IV

That all tomorrows have no wound in store
      For shrinking Joy, nor any prick of dread,
I know, who closed its eyes forevermore,
      And keep this night a vigil with my dead.

This little space my out-thrown hands have stirred
      Is happy earth, for once it knew love's feet;
Here once love stood and called the heart that heard,
      And all the garden, all the world, grew sweet.

I lay my joy within this hollowed space
      (I had not thought so blithe a thing could die!)
And heap the happy earth upon the face
      That has no will to smile nor breath to sigh.

With dew beneath and hushing night above
      I cannot tell how long my grief has lain—
Virgin, I will not plead you for my love,
      Only the pain,—if you would ease the pain.

V

The world below was deep in stormy cloud;
>But high in sun we flew along the ledge,
And to the strength I rode I cried aloud
>And spurred it near against the trembling edge.

(I rode Ramon along the mountain wall.
>Today he had no wilder mood than I—
No wilder will for lawless wind to call
>Upon the narrow trail that meets the sky.)

The sharp air flowed like water through my hands.
>Heart, how I skirted death and laughed at pain!
Forgotten pain in half-remembered lands
>Below me in the valleys with the rain.

VI

What alters with my changing? Not José,
      Content in little duties that he loves.
Not Marta's dimming eyes that stare away
      Beyond the tranquil court, the circling doves.

I, too, I float on peace, forget almost,
      And then as drowning sight may pierce the sea
To find the sun a green and wavering ghost,
      And shapes of earth distorted monstrously,—

I see a mocking earth, a sun distraught,
      I lose the buoying instant of relief
And sink again as wearying soul and thought
      Drown in the sick amazement of my grief.

VII

I tilt my hollowed life and look within;
        The wine it held has left a purple trace—
Behold, a stain where happiness had been.
        If I should shatter down this empty vase,

Through what abysses would my soul be tossed
        To meet its judge in undiscovered lands?
What sentence meted me, alone and lost,
        Before him with the fragments in my hands?

Better the patient earth that loves me still
        Should drip her clearness on this purple stain;
Better my life upheld to her should fill
        With limpid dew, and gradual gift of rain.

VIII

Some whim of Marta's shields me from the night,
    And fretted that my curtain should be kept
Close drawn, and wakeful candles over bright,
    I welcomed in the quiet moon and slept;

Then woke again in fear—the night was old,
    The witching tide of silver shut away,
And Marta's shaking hand on mine was cold,
    Her bending face above me strange and grey.

"Who sleeps beneath the moon," she whispered low,
    "Must pale with her, nor wind nor noon-day sky
Be his again whose pulses beat more slow,
    More faint, till with the waning moon . . . they die."

THE END

The Garden of Dolores

The garden of Dolores! Here she walked.
      When fretted in the twilight's pallid space
      The trees were black and delicate as lace,
And palms were etchings, sharp and slender-stalked.

Now riots summer in these magic closes,
      And life is rounded in the frailest spray. . . .
      Dolores, cold and buried yesterday,
Is it thy spirit here among the roses?

For restless murmurs through the garden seek;
      To shadowy caress the flowers unclose;
      A blossom in the dark magnolia glows—
Or leaning pallor of an oval cheek?

Upon the dusk is borne a strange long cry,
      And one quick sob of wind the air has moved.
      Ah, perfect garden that Dolores loved,
Her soul has called to thee . . . a far goodbye.

Answered

The moon crept in and found her dead,
The moon crept in upon our tears;
"O life of idle days!" we said,
"O short young life of wasted years!
That Death should close the laughing eyes,
And still the lips before we knew
If through her girlhood's mysteries
Shone aught of purpose strong and true."

The Spring came to her where she slept—
"In flowers her nature blooms," we thought;
For slender daisies round her crept,
Gay, with her careless beauty fraught.
But strange! we saw them with a start,
We saw, and as we looked we knew—
For there above the girlish heart,
With upturned faces, pansies grew.

INDIFFERENCE

There is a thread from you to me?
      I know, I feel it drawing still,
A cobweb on my careless thought—
      Old habit-likeness—what you will.

Because it once was strong as Fate
      To bind a life to your desire,—
Because its knots about my heart
      Could burn me like a witch's wire,

You will not think it loosed. And I
      (Ah, woman soul that prayed "Destroy!")
Free from the fretting of my pain,
      Have killed the fitful strength of joy.

After-Knowledge

You found my soul an untried instrument.
    I closed it fast and bade you take the key,
Serene in my unquestioning content
    That you alone could wake the harmony.

I gave the key, indifferent though it cost.
    Familiar lightness of unskilful touch,
The music to the master. If I lost,
    He lets the little go who profits much.

Ah, then the keen, reluctant knowledge grew
    That though the chords were helpless at your will
You had nor wit nor power to sound them true:
    Discordant they, or else forever still.

BE SILENT, LOVE

Be silent, love. I will not have you speak;
    While weary tongues may falter, speech endures.
This only dies:—Your lips upon my cheek,
    The wonder of my eyes asleep on yours.

I will not that we barter pebbles tossed,
    To wave-worn shores by sea on sea of men.
This blossom of the moment born and lost,
    Is wholly ours and not to live again.

All moulded words another breast must grace,
    As down the years indifferent jewels shine.
But none may share the silence of your face
    Down bending to the lifted kiss of mine.

Two Spendthrift Kings

These tawny sheaves, this fragrant land,
    Two spendthrift kings have found and seized,
And Vagabondia may demand
    Its pockets lined, its troubles eased.

We hold or deed as fancy wills.
    We own the world by right and law—
The hidden gold in all the hills,
    The sweetness in a yellow straw.

GROWTH

I twine you, little trellis, close and fond,
And swing in wistful threads above, beyond,
For air and space to blossom. Be it so.
Ah me! I love you, but the plant must grow.

I quiver with the call of summer heat,
With all the wild sap stirring at my feet.
My quiet trellis, impotent to know
The earth and sun command me: I must grow.

You cannot share my ardent life apart,
Nor feel the upward straining of my heart.
In every vein the urging currents flow,
Leaf after leaf unfolds: the plant must grow.

Change

Beloved, have I turned indeed so cold?
    My eyes are faithful, grieving with your grief;
And if the year itself could grow not old,
    Could stand at waking sap and budding leaf,

An April heart might keep its first unrest,
    An April love the petals of its spring.
When all the birds are silent in my breast,
    How can I answer when you bid me sing?

The autumn hills are brown: you will not see.
    The saddened woodland speaks, and finds you strange.
Ah, dear one, all my world is kin to me,
    And with the swerving days I change, I change.

WISTARIA

The blue wistaria hangs with bloom
The Place of Memories far away.
My heart has ached with it today—
The blue wistaria is in bloom.

And one may pass so near, so near,
With half-remembering eyes and cold,
Where quickening with the budding year
It clusters perfect as of old;

And one at sight of wizened sprays,
Reluctant in an alien spring,
Must feel the sharp, unblunted sting,
The pang of unforgotten days.

How Ends the Day?

We wandered where the violets bloom, beside the sunlit stream.
We saw, where on the crystal waves, the water lilies dream.
Their gold hearts wreathed in leaves of pearl, all silvered by the sun,
We heard the brook laugh as it swayed their bright heads one by one;
Yet no smile dawned upon your face, to chase the tears away.
"The waters cease, the lilies fade, in darkness ends the day."

We walked through paths where gleams of light like gold through green leaves came,
Where darts down through the shadowy boughs the oriole's flash of flame;
We listened where the voice of birds swells out in chorus strong;
How the rippling notes of gladness poured forth its glorious song!
But answering joy woke not in you, you saw but shadows gray.
"The sunshine fades and beauty flees, in sorrow ends the day."

We lingered where the pine trees lift their branches dark on high,
A song of deep content they sing beneath the sunny sky;
Their low continuous murmur falls upon the soul like balm.
And tears and sorrow have no place within their solemn calm.
But that dark shadow from your brow, no sound could drive away,
"Our life is short, and all things die, in weeping ends the day."

But soft from out the velvet grass, the dewdrops gleaming bright,
An Easter lily, white and gold, stands queenly in the light;
Its purity recalls sweet words of everlasting peace,
Of one, who, dying long ago, bade all our sorrows cease:
A smile like sunshine lights your face, its sadness flees away.
"Though we must die, we live again, in glory ends the day."

My Nook

Oh, half way up the hill it was, where one might sit leaf-hidden,
    And stare across the canyoned depths to distant miles of blue;
Upon the little path to it no foot might step unbidden.
    It was my nook, and mine alone, and not another knew.

And when my doll was sawdust, or my little hopes were fated,
    Or all my world was shaken by a little idol's fall,
Up to my dear retreat I'd climb, with grief or anger weighted,
    And, hands behind fern-pillowed head, straightway forget it all.

With tears yet damp upon my cheeks I'd fall to castle-building
    (The careless linnets fluttered near a little maid so still),
And all the gorgeous tints I knew, and all the wealth of gilding,
    Were lavished on the future that I summoned there at will.

"When one is small the troubles come, and then the tears must follow;
    When one is small one finds it good to run and cry alone,
But I shall laugh to think that once I found my world so hollow—
    I shall not need this little nook," I thought, "When I am grown."

Now heart whose voice I drown by day to hear in hours of waking,
    Now eyes whose tears must burn the more because they may not flow,
From sight of face or sound of speech if I could bear your aching,
    And bury it deep-hidden in the ferns of long ago!

But oh! the pensive little ghost among her visions sitting
    Would view her weeping Future with so piteous surprise!
No, I must leave her in her nook to dream her dreams unwitting—
    I could not take my trouble there, I could not meet her eyes.

When Plaintively and Near the Cricket Sings

Now evening comes. Now stirs my discontent . . .
    Oh, ache of smallest, unforgotten things!
How sharp you are when day and dark are blent,
      When beetles hurry by with vibrant wings,
      And plaintively and near the cricket sings.

The sighing garden calls me from the door;
      Above the hills a little crescent swings—
Above the path where you will come no more
      When beetles hurry by on vibrant wings,
      And plaintively and near the cricket sings.

The Little Memories

My thoughts of you . . . although I strain and sigh
    At stubborn roots, at boughs that tear my face,
No plants in all my garden grow so high,
    Nor fill with sturdier life a wider place.

It pleases me, and wakes an old delight,
    To go with wordy shears in idle times
And trim them as a patient gardener might,
    Clipping the thorny boughs to curves and rhymes.

If these were all, opposing strength with strength
    To make my hurt an easier thing to bear;
If these alone usurped my garden's length,
    It would not be so hard—I should not care.

But close against the ground, oh, small and weak!
    The trodden flowers, the little memories, grow.
Uprooting fingers press them to my cheek. . . .
    Dear heart, I love you, and I miss you so.

Pass By

Mind said, "Pass by.
The garden withers, for the spring is dry.
For words of thine, for tears, it will not flow.
The long road calls a wanderer: rise and go."

Heart said, "Pass by.
The flowers were pale and scentless; let them die,
And down the road Forget your pathway take
To find beneath the Song my fine, small ache,
And gather flowers blue and flowers red
To hear my whisper of the white ones dead."

In Empty Courts

His love is warm and constant as the sun,
    Like sunlight in the outer spaces spent,
In empty courts where tumbling fountains run,
    And flowers bloom, and he is well content.

To you my heart must turn for all its light—
    Alas, the grudging taper that you give!
So small to make the inner temple bright,
    So dim to give the glow by which I live.

He is the sun, for all the world to mark,
    So warm and fair he shines! nor understands
That I must still be crouching in the dark,
    Shielding a little flame with loving hands.

Down the Trail

Break camp, the dawn is here!
A sea has swept beneath us in the night—
Poured outward in a wrinkled floor of white,
And left our eyrie clear.
There in the deeps the little trail is curled—
We plunge like divers to the under-world.

The manzanita stirs!
Look, in that little thicket just ahead!
Down, down, the covey whirrs,
Mocking us, careful, led,
Slow-slipping beads along a slender thread.

Here the stream flows;
Here we tread yellow leaves.
(Sun in the sycamores,
Sun on the granite walls.)
All is so still,
Never wind blows,
Only the singing stream
Shouts little waterfalls.

We round the mighty shoulder of a hill—
Oh, sweet airs damp with ferns!
The day is old, the lengthening shadows chill—
The wanderer returns.

Traffic, and wakeful eyes of little lights;
The black crowd passing near; and far away
A fading rose of sunset hanging low
Above the roofs of indigo and grey.

"Bells from Over the Hills Sound Sweet"
—Russian Proverb.

Oh, when the afternoon is long and hazy,
    So still the valley lies, so still, so still,
With sweeping smoky spirals blue and lazy,
    With yellow light aglow from hill to hill.
Sometimes the echoes startle with my singing;
    Sometimes a bird the heavy silence fills,
And always I can hear them ringing, ringing,
    My mocking bells, my Bells from over the Hills.

Sweetly, faintly ring they, cruel ring they:
    "Captive in your prison, hear us call!"
Message from a life of action bring they,
    Life beyond these hills more sweet than all.
Would that I could heed their call and follow,
    Waking while this drowsy valley sleeps,
Follow Fortune over hill and hollow,
    Wrest from her the treasures that she keeps!

My freedom gained, what fate would be for telling?
    Still hills and hills beyond would stretch for aye.
Peace in this little valley has its dwelling,
    And that the chase would profit, who shall say?

For hopes and dear delights, ah, who can near them?
    Something ungained, the heart with longing fills,
And follow though I might, I still should hear them,
    The mocking bells, the Bells from over the Hills.

In Town

The long street where the people go—
It is not like the paths I know,
Yet can I find the morning there,
All crystal light and early air.

Sharp-angled roofs in slanting sun
Grow dimmer as they slope and blend,
Until they crowd no more, and one
May see his mountains at the end.

Then, when the day has had her will,
I lean upon my window-sill,
And watch them floating, clean and high—
My sunset ships across the sky.

Moods

I

Sweet grasses, tasseled, bent and tall;
    And sweet last light across the meadow—
The wind has tangled, left them all
    In webs of green, in silver shadow.

And to your speech my heart replies,
    Still silvering to each word that passes,
Until a tangled joy it lies,
    A shining web of wind-blown grasses.

II

A memory of tears that day,
    Of small and piteous lives misused:
The fallen bird we could not save,
    The butterfly we helped—and bruised.

And last, to fill repentant eyes,
    Most bright and frail of winged things—
A moment's faith, an hour's love,
    Grieving the dust with broken wings.

A Misty Morning

Low-arched above me as I moved the hollowed air was clear;
Beyond was whiteness dim and strange, and spectral shapes drew near.
Upon the little shore of brown that touched the misty sea,
Upon the shadowy borderland, one paused and looked at me;
Then hurried on with greeting smile and sudden vivid face:
A friend had started into life within my magic space!
Into the world of ghosts again I watched him fade away—
First black he was, then dim he was, then merged in formless grey.

Two Songs

You love the chant of green,
    The low-voiced trees, the meadow's monotone.
        O friend of mine, it is for these you pray.
This alien land must call unheard, unseen,
    While one beloved note your heart has known,
        To hunger for it, half a world away.

Come with me to my height,
    And stand at sunset when the winds are still,
        Watching the hollow valleys brim with light,
The red and brown and yellow hills—they shout,
    And on the shoulders of the marching host
        The bayonets are gleaming points of white.

Pressing beyond to deep and gradual blues,
    Their lessening voices die in distance pale—
        Ineffably dissolved in opal hues;
Against the sky the last sweet echoes fail
    While all the West is quivering, fold on fold
        To one great voice—one vibrant peal of gold.

Noon

The brook flowed through a bending arch of leaves—
Flowed through an arch of leaves into the sun;
But all was shadow where it left my feet—
A shade with netted ripples overrun,
A brook that flowed in coolness to the sun.

Beyond the arch of shadow color lay—
Vivid to narrowed eyelids, fiercely bright,
And bright the happy water slipped away
In gleaming pools and broken lines of light.

Your Beautiful Passing

Across my thought has trailed your beautiful passing,
As a wild bird ruffles the motionless brink of the water,
Moving in gradual path on its mirror of shadow,
After him streaking and trembling long ripples of silver.

By Moonlight

Is this the world I knew? Beneath the day
It glowed with golden heat, with vivid hues—
Mountains and sky that merged in melting blues
And hazy air that shimmered far away.

This world is white beneath a silver sky—
White with pale brightness, luminously chill.
The moon reigns queen, but faintly shining still
The dim stars glimmer on the hilltops high.

Here, where long grasses touch across the stream
That threads with babbling laugh its narrow way,
My face turned upward to pale gleams that stray
Through whispering willow boughs . . . I dream and dream.

A Dream-Love

Ah, happier he who gains not
The love some seem to gain,
The joy that custom stains not
Shall still with him remain,
The loveliness that wanes not,
The love that ne'er can wane.

In dreams she grows not older,
The land of dreams among,
Though all the world wax colder,
Though all the songs be sung,
In dreams doth he behold her
Still fair and kind and young.

One Day

The levels where the trail began
Were sown with silver-grey.
We bruised the leaves with hurrying feet
To wafts of strong and tarry sweet,
A moment's pleasure as we ran,
Forgotten on our way.

Above, along the farthest crest,
In every brief and breathless rest
The spice of sage was ours,
Crushed from the dull and slender leaves—
The tiny yellow flowers,
When day was done
No more remembered than the wind and sun.

The Mission Graves

By man forgotten,
Nature remembers, with her fitful tears.
The wooden slabs lose name and date with years,
And crumble, rotten.

The Padre there,
On Saint's day, from an evening rite returning,
Set for each unknown soul a candle burning,
With muttered prayer.

Glow-worms, they shone—
Strange, spectral-gleaming through the lonely dark.
Whose nameless dust did each faint glimmer mark—
Skull, crumbling bone?

Ah, the Dead knew!
The grateful Dead, far-called from voids of space,
Each by the tiny spark that gave him grace,
Watched, the night through.

ALONG THE TRACK

The track has led me out beyond the town
    To follow day across the waning fields,
The crisping weeds and wastes of tender brown.

On either side the feathered tops are high,
    A tracery of broken arabesques
Upon the sullen crimson of the sky.

Into the west the narrowing rails are sped.
    They cut the crayon softness of the dusk
With thin converging gleams of bloody red.

A Place of Dreams

Here will we drink content, comrade of mine—
    Here, where the little stream, to meet the sun,
Flows down a yellow rock like yellow wine.

Here will we launch a leaf to distant shores,
    And in it shut a word for Wonderland—
The blue Unknown beyond the sycamores.

Think Not, O Lilias

Think not, O Lilias, that the love of this night will endure in the sun. Hast thou beheld fungi, white, evil, rosy-lined, poisonous, shrivel in the eyes of day?

In this wilderness of strange hearts it is not thine alone that concerns me. Many brave hearts of men are more to me than thine. The hearts of men breathe deeply. As for thy heart, it runs from me, it is quicksilver, it does not concern me greatly.

The Suicide

The sleepless night had been a whirl of aching memory and self-hatred, huge chaotic fancies and plunges in a clotted swamp where a lake had been laughter-fed by brooks of sanity. His body had fought for its life against his brain.

There was knowledge in his very flesh of effort and weariness, heat and cold, the brush of wet reeds, the shock of a wave, the bite of a hill wind. No glory of color, no softness of touch or sweetness of scent that the man's life had known but worked on its particular sense and cried out. His body was a whimpering Earth Giant that the dominating brain was bent on swinging into nothingness, as Hercules held Anteus away from the touch of his mother until he died.

Curiously enough the man had no regret for his body. Detail by detail he planned its destruction. He loved his brain. Even as he used one deliberate thought tool after another, he laid each down caressingly. "All these will be broken," said his consciousness. "Something will live," argued the man. "But this will never have a head, or that arms."

"To Rosy Buds..."

To rosy buds in orchards of the spring,
    To melting clouds in endless deeps of air,
My love shall lift a swelling throat and sing,
    Akin to all things fugitive and fair.

They shut love from his heaven and he sings?
    But captive eyes are pitiful to see!
Oh, flashing sun on upward-beating wings—
    Oh, tumbling notes of joy—my bird is free!

Dear love, forever strange, beloved most!
    Dear fleeting buds, bear not your fruit and die!
Be this a path forever found and lost,
    A drift of bloom upon an April sky.

Yesterday

Now all my thoughts were crisped and thinned
    To elfin threads, to gleaming browns.
Like tawny grasses lean with wind
    They drew your heart across the downs.
Your will of all the winds that blew
    They drew across the world to me,
To thread my whimsey thoughts of you
    Along the downs, above the sea.

Beneath a pool beyond the dune—
    So green it was and amber-walled
A face would glimmer like a moon
    Seen whitely through an emerald—
And there my mermaid fancy lay
    And dreamed the light and you were one,
And flickered in her sea-weed's sway
    A broken largesse of the sun.

Above the world as evening fell
    I made my heart into a sky,
And through a twilight like a shell
    I saw the shining sea-gulls fly.
I found between the sea and land
    And lost again, unwrit, unheard,
A song that fluttered in my hand
    And vanished like a silver bird.

The Mourner

Because my love has wave and foam for speech,
    And never words, and yearns as water grieves,
With white arms curving on a listless beach,
    And murmurs inarticulate as leaves—

I am become beloved of the night—
    Her huge sea-lands ineffable and far
Hold crouched and splendid Sorrow, eyed with light,
    And Pain who beads his forehead with a star.

Ave atque Vale

It gathers where the moody sky is bending;
    It stirs the air along familiar ways—
A sigh for strange things dear forever ending,
    For beauty shrinking in these alien days.

Now nothing is the same, old visions move me:
    I wander silent through the waning land,
And find for youth and little leaves to love me
    The old, old lichen crumbling in my hand.

What shifting films of distance fold you, blind you,
    This windy eve of dreams, I cannot tell.
I know they grope through some strange mist to find you,
    My hands that give you Greeting and Farewell.

At the End

Tremblingly and spent I ran and fell,
And ran again, a sorrow made me fleet.
For very fear its shape I could not tell—
    The briars tore my feet.

In broken flight across the cruel land,
So weary was I that I only smiled
When, swift and strong, a tender, mighty hand
    Upraised me like a child.

"It was not you I feared," rejoiced, I cried,
(His touch had healed my hurts, no more they bled,)
"Life radiant, God has sent you to my side!"
    "Nay, I am Death!" he said.

Notes

ORIGINAL NOTES (1910)

["The Outer Gate."] This poem, so distinctly prophetic, was written a year and four months before her death.

"The Rose" was written for Mr. Porter Garnett on the occasion of his marriage.

"The Message." These lines were in response to a long telegram dispatched at night by a distant friend.

Of the poem, "Just a Dog," a letter says: "My cousin, who used often to play on the piano, died; and after his death his dog, when anyone touched the instrument, used to come from wherever he might be to see if the player were not his master. Then he would slink away again. The dog died after a few grieving months. I loved him, and made these verses."

"Mirage" is an endeavor to portray the alien attitude of one who had long vainly sought love.

"My Nook" was written at the age of sixteen.

"Think Not, O Lilias." These prose lines were recalled out of a dream. They are included here because of their singular beauty.

"Yesterday," and "The Mourner" which follows it, are the last poems. "Ave atque Vale" was written some two years before.

The responsibility for these notes lies with Mr. Henry Anderson Lafler, who has edited this book. Thanks are due to Mr. George Sterling and Mr. Porter Garnett, who have lightened the labor of its preparation.

ADDITIONAL NOTES

Most of the general information concerning the approximate dates of creation, composition, or publication for many of the poems is taken from "The Life and Writings of Nora May French," by Judith Allen, her M.A. thesis done for the English Department of Mills College, Oakland, 1963.

"The Rose." Probably June 1907 or somewhat before.

"By the Hospital." Probably 1901 or somewhat later. The French family was residing at this time not far from the general or county hospital in or near what is now downtown Los Angeles, having moved there from Glendale.

"My Maid of Dreams." Published in the *Los Angeles Times* (19 February 1900). Signed "Nora May French." A rather subtle portrait of Persephone or Proserpine.

"Music in the Pavilion." Sometime in 1899.

"In Camp." Written during the summer of 1906.

"The Nymph." Sometime before "The Spanish Girl." These are Nora May's only (two) surviving narrative poems.

"Vivisection." Probably 1901 or somewhat later. See the note for "By the Hospital."

"The Lost Chimneys." Published in *Sunset* (December 1906).

"San Francisco, New Year's, 1907." Published *San Francisco Call* (1 January 1907), under the title "Says the Old Year to the New." Republished in *Current Literature* (June 1908), under the same title.

"The Panther Woman." Sometime September–November 1907. One of Nora May's last poems. (Bancroft Library.)

"Poppies." Hitherto unheralded and unpublished. (Bancroft Library.) No date, but at least before September 1906, and possibly the spring or early summer of that year. The poem is handwritten on a sheet of stationery printed with the name of the Hotel Nadeau, Los Angeles, California, at the top. It is signed "Nora French."

"Mirage." Published in *Sunset* (October 1907).

"The Spanish Girl." Parts I and II, sometime around 1903. Part III, created or completed sometime during the winter of 1905–06. Part II, Poem VII appeared as "Happiness" in the *American Magazine* (June 1908). Although Nora May places the story in the California of the Spanish Colonial period (probably the first half of the nineteenth century), it is noteworthy that she does not entitle it "The Mexican Girl."

"Answered." According to Judith Allen, pansies growing from the grave of an inexperienced girl symbolize a heart at peace. The word itself derives directly from the French *pensée*, meaning thought, concept, idea, judgment, opinion, fancy.

"Be Silent, Love." Sometime around 1903.

"Change." Sometime late summer of 1907.

"How Ends the Day?" Published in the *Los Angeles Times* (20 May 1894). Signed "Nora French." Earliest known surviving poem. Discovered and made available on the Internet by Pamela Herr. Published just after Nora May's thirteenth birthday on 26 April 1894, but probably created when she was twelve, the age at which she began writing both prose and poetry. Not only an unusually pensive composition by a twelve-year-old, but a remarkably sustained performance for a person of that age.

"A Dream-Love." Late August 1906. (Bancroft Library.)

"The Suicide." Nora May probably created this, her only other known poem in prose and one of her last pieces, sometime during the first half of November 1907. (Bancroft Library.)

"Ave atque Vale." Published in *Sunset*, probably December 1907.

"At the End." Dated in pencil "1903"—possibly by Helen French Hunt. (Bancroft Library.)

The order of arrangement for the titles of the following poems reflects their order in the contents of the main text.

1899–1905: These twelve poems appeared in *Out West*, edited by Charles Lummis; hence, Nora May created them sometime during this overall period: "By the Hospital," "The Constant Ones," "Summer Dusk" [as "Dusk"], "The Old Garden" ["The Spanish Girl," Part I, Poem III: "The Garden"], "Answered," "Down the Trail," "Mist" ["A Misty Morning"], "Two Songs," "By Moonlight," "One Day," "The Mission Graves," "Along the Track." (Only "Answered" remained uncollected in *Poems*.)

Around 1904–06: "The Message," "The Spanish Girl, Part III," "Be Silent, Love," "Ave atque Vale." ("Remembered," also created at this same general time, is apparently lost, unless it is a known poem but under an otherwise unrecorded title.)

Notices

General Note

Not many people have written concerning Nora May French, her life, death, and poetry. Therefore it serves a real purpose, and addresses a genuine lack, to gather these rare but public documents concerning Nora May's life and work. This appendix brings together such materials, or the more outstanding of them. The term "notices," as employed here, covers longer notes, news articles and other items, appraisals, appreciations, and reviews, some mentioned in the biographical-critical introduction to this volume, and some already quoted in part. The long article in the *San Francisco Examiner* for Friday, 15 November 1907, ranks in particular as a kind of self-conscious masterpiece in the yellow-journalism style prevalent in the latter nineteenth and early twentieth century in this country. The order of the materials is more or less chronological. The lack of a regular or conventional bibliography of all Nora May's writings, published or unpublished, renders the task of dealing with her extant output in verse and in prose far more difficult and complex than it would otherwise be.

San Francisco Bulletin, Friday evening, 15 November 1907.
BEAUTIFUL POETESS TAKES HER LIFE AT HOME OF STERLING
Nora French Finds Death by Poison. [no portrait.] from p. 3.

With the lonely ocean moaning down the shore-line below George Sterling's bungalow perched among the murmuring pines of Carmel-by-the-Sea, Nora May French, poetess, dreamer and beauty, rose from her uneasy bed in her brother poet's home Wednesday at midnight, mixed a swift and subtle poison and drinking, lay down again to die. When Mrs. Sterling hurried from her room to answer the guttural cry that echoed through the house there was a sick foam on the girl's pale lips and in a little while, with no message to those she left, she had passed on to the land of her heart's desire.

Nora French was in love with death. She courted it as a lover and found it in the night-time when all weird shadows throng to the bedside of the introspective. In the glad day and glorious change of shifting color with which afternoon invests Carmel she had sought her strange companion, but missed him by the very life that pulsed in her veins.

WAITS IN SHADOW

Two days before she died she made a tryst with death and shot away one lock of the bright hair which aureoled her delicate face. Her uncle, a Presbyterian minister, had often talked to her of self-destruction, telling her to stay pistol in hand, in the path of a shadow, and shoot when the edge of the soft gloom reached her. This, he said, would cure her of her desire. But the idea fascinated the girl.

Monday she sat in the Sterling cottage, where she was a visitor, and brooded over a verse in Housman's "Shropshire Lad" in which a youth ends his life with a revolver. Below the lines she wrote, "Bravely done, my lad; bravely done," and then, with Sterling's revolver concealed in her dress, glided out to a quiet place in the sun on which the shadows are encroaching.

With nerves at a steel tension she waited the approach of the shadow, and when Death's herald touched the edge of her garments she shot. But her hand was less steady than she thought and the ball sped past her head, cropping one vagrant strand of hair. At this outcome her mood changed and, returning, she laughingly rehearsed her experience to Mrs. Sterling, showed her the shorn lock of hair and blessed her uncle for his advice. It had cured her, she declared.

TRAGEDY IN PLOT

Perhaps Miss French did not know it, but she had wooed death too sweetly for him to give her up. Mary Austin, the novelist and one of the colony at Carmel, is working on a volume in which the heroine solves her problems with cyanide of potassium. The poison appealed to Miss French; she made enquiries about it, learned its virulence and finally procured some from Dr. Beck, saying, with pathetic cunning, that she wished it to clean silver.

This is what she mixed and drank when Mrs. Sterling responded to her suppressed choking. The tender woman, whose poet-husband was away, found the girl in what she supposed was an attack of hysterics.

"Now, Nora May, you be good," Mrs. Sterling said as she snuggled into bed beside her friend. But the body of Miss French grew chiller and chiller, and finally the watcher saw in the gleam of the night-lamp a glass with white sediment on the table. Frightened, she rushed to the bungalow of Jimmy Hopper and Fred Bechdolt, who are collaborating at Carmel. When the three returned the unhappy poetess had been dead some time.

EXPLANATION LACKING

No reasonable motive seems to account for the tragedy. A telegram from her sister in Los Angeles reveals that she had suffered three operations and anticipated another, but she went to Carmel for her health and seemed to be unusually rosy and robust for her. She appeared strangely indifferent to men, though it is said she was engaged to a young Englishman and had left a broken heart behind her in San Francisco with one of the Bohemian poets.

The work of the dead girl foreshadowed as much promise as that of any literary woman on the coast. Her output was small but choice, and always had the glamour of true poetry—the dynamic phrase, the intimate thought. Her prose was vigorous and graceful as appears by her "Diary of a Telephone Girl," recently developed from her own experience and published in the *Saturday Evening Post*.

Miss French, who was only 26 years old, came from Los Angeles, where her father is one of the officials of the Old Soldiers' Home near Santa Monica. With her sister, Helen, she reached San Francisco shortly after the fire, and for a time they lived in a cottage on Russian Hill owned by Henry Anderson Lafler, himself a poet and the editor of the Blue Mule. Her fresh and spiritual beauty made her a welcome guest at all the foregatherings of the Bohemian set, where it was soon learned that she had extraordinary talent.

Among her effects was found a short verse, which she had entitled, "Ave atque Vale." Perhaps it was written to the ghostly lover that she sought. The last stanza reads:

[The stanza in question is the same as in the *Poems* of 1910.]

N.B. It is possible that the three operations mentioned uniquely in this obituary (that is, nowhere else), plus the possibility of a fourth, could all refer to abortions, however induced or otherwise realized.

San Francisco Call, Friday, 15 November 1907.

[The article is accompanied by the now standard portrait by Arnold Genthe on the frontispiece of *Poems*. Underneath the photograph reads the following: Nora May French, gifted writer, who committed suicide in Sterling bungalow at Carmel by taking cyanide of potassium.]

NORA MAY FRENCH, WRITER, ENDS LIFE WITH POISON
Friend Has Telepathic Vision of the Poet's Death Scene

A telegram was received from Monterey last night, stating that Nora May French, a writer well known in this city, had committed suicide by taking cyanide of potassium in the bungalow of the poet, George Sterling. He was away from home, and it was Mrs. Sterling who, hearing groans, went to the apartment occupied by Miss French and found her dying. On the table near at hand was a small box of cyanide of potassium which she had procured the day before for the ostensible purpose of cleaning silver. Help was summoned, but before a doctor arrived the girl was dead. A verdict of suicide was entered at a coroner's inquest held yesterday afternoon. No reason is known for the suicide.

Miss French had been living for two weeks with the Sterlings, having gone to the country to have a better opportunity to write. She was 24 years of age and came here from Los Angeles some two years ago with her sister, Helen French Hunt. She has a brother and a father in Los Angeles. Upon receipt of the telegram announcing her death George Sterling, who was here, left for Carmel, accompanied by Henry A. Lafler, one of the group of friends with whom Miss French was intimately acquainted.

While dying at Carmel in the midnight hour Thursday morning Miss French sent a telepathic message to an intimate friend in San Francisco. This friend, whose veracity cannot be questioned, saw the act in a dream—saw the potion lifted to the girl's lips, and saw her writhing in the death agony. It is firmly believed by the one who dreamed of the act of suicide that the vision came at the moment when Nora French, moved by some impulse which is not understood by her friends, ended a life that gave great promise.

Nora May French was a poet of rare talent. Her output was small, but everything that she had written was invested with haunting beauty. George Sterling has said of her that whenever she put her pen to paper something perfect was the result. She could not write anything commonplace, he said. That she might be free to write as she chose, she went, two weeks ago, to live with Mr. and Mrs. Sterling at their cottage at Carmel. It was remarked by a friend at about the time that she left, that suicide would be her end, but the idea was scoffed at by her intimates.

Until two weeks ago Miss French and her sister, Helen, lived at 415 Lombard Street in a bungalow owned by Henry A. Lafler, and now occupied by Mr. and Mrs. Perry Newberry. While here Miss French was one of the literary and artistic coterie composed of Lafler, Porter Garnett, Gelett Burgess,

Xavier Martinez, George Sterling, Herman Whitaker and others. She was employed for a time by the Pacific States telephone company and was the author of "The Diary of a Telephone Girl," which appeared in the Saturday Evening Post a few weeks ago, and which, as it was based on the recent telephone girls' strike here, created considerable local interest. A few touches were put to the article by Gelett Burgess, but in all its essentials it was the work of Miss French.

Miss French was a frail girl—of striking appearance, and one who exercised a charm over all the men she met. They made no impression on her, however, it being apparent that her chief object in associating with them was to make a psychological study of them. She was of an exceedingly nervous temperament, and ordinarily gave no sign of talent. It was only those who knew her well to whom the brilliancy of her mind was apparent.

For some four years she had been contributing to the various coast magazines, and some of her verse had found its way into eastern publications. She had a sure and beautiful touch in her work and wrote with rare felicity of the moods of nature. The swirl of the rain, the whisper of the wind in the tule-grasses, bird song and the calm, sweet freshness of early morning—the themes that poets have used for thousands of years—were her themes. She wrote of these things with a sympathy, understanding and melody surpassed by few. To quote from one of her recent, and by no means one of her best, poems:

> "It is a silver space between two rains;
> The lulling storm has given to the day
> An hour of windless air and riven grey;
> The world is drained of color; light remains."

This and other things that she had done will be treasured as expressions of a woman more than ordinarily gifted.

* * *

N.B. About two thirds through the article appears the poem "Says the Old Year to the New" under its later title "San Francisco, New Year's, 1907"—almost identical with the version in *Poems*. The one real difference occurs in line 16 beginning "I filled the night," which here begins "Yes, I filled the night, etc." The following caption appears before the poem, sic:

> The following poem, ushering in the present year, was written by Nora May French for the Sunday Call of December 20, 1906, and in vigorous lan-

guage she tells of the year of the disaster coming in with smiles and departing amid terror and tears:

San Francisco Chronicle, Friday, 15 November 1907.

NORA MAY FRENCH, POETESS, ENDS LIFE BY TAKING POISON TALENT AND BEAUTY HERS; MOTIVE UNKNOWN

One of the Elect in the Local Colony of Artists and Writers.

BRILLIANT FUTURE AWAITED

Takes Cyanide of Potassium at Bungalow of Poet Sterling.

There has passed from the realm of Bohemia one of its fairest flowers, and in all the gay haunts where the elite of the literary and artistic world are wont to gather voices were hushed last night and tears dimmed the eyes of the diners. The red wine was left untasted in the cups and the sound of laughter did not echo from the tables where poet and painter nightly assemble to indulge in the feast of reason and flow of soul.

Nora May French, poetess and author, beloved for her scintillating spirits, her wit, her talent and her beauty in that elect coterie of Bohemians that knows Harry A. Lafler, Gelett Burgess, Xavier Martinez, the Perry Newberrys, the Colonel Edwin Emersons and others, ended her life early yesterday morning by swallowing a quantity of cyanide of potassium at the bungalow of Poet George F. Sterling at Carmel-by-the-Sea. The Sterling bungalow is the center of artistic life in the picturesque colony below Monterey, and Miss French had been there for some days as the guest of Mrs. Sterling.

AT LOSS TO EXPLAIN MOTIVE

This talented young woman, whose life seemed full of hope and promise, for whom friends predicted a most brilliant career, elected to take her own life in the most tragic, sudden and inexplicable manner. Whether her act was merely the result of sudden suicidal impulse, or whether it was committed after long brooding and deliberation in a moment of despair and desperation, none of her friends can conjecture. All of her friends are profoundly shocked at the sad tragedy and are at a loss to explain the impulse that prompted her rash act, for while those who knew her best know that she was the heroine of more than one heart dalliance, they were certain, despite the morose tone of some of her late poems, that she found in life a welcoming career and the prospect of a brilliant future. Among those who admired her talents to the point of devotion was Harry A. Lafler, littérateur, editor of the Blue Mule, and acknowledged leader of the Bohemian colony that has made Telegraph Hill a name to conjure with and has pictured the joy of living on the lengthy walls of a Pine street cafe where it holds nightly revel. A short time ago Lafler was granted a divorce, and since then friends of Miss French have playfully twitted her about a rumor that said that she would soon announce her engagement to Lafler. But the fair poetess denied the soft impeachment and insisted that she was devoted only to her art. Lafler was one of the first to hurry to the deathbed of the young poetess when news of the sad event reached this city.

HIGH LITERARY AMBITION

Miss French was intensely ambitious. Her struggle for recognition as a poetess is said by some to have embittered her against life, not a little. It was only recently that the editors of the magazines saw her genius and her work found ready acceptance. At one time she almost gave up the fight and sought employment as a telephone operator. She worked in the Sutter street exchange of the Pacific States Company for several months, but resigned her position about a year ago and since that time she has devoted herself exclusively to literary work. Her poems have been published in "The Sunset Magazine" and other local periodicals, while some of her short stories have appeared in Eastern publications. One of these stories, "The Confessions of a Telephone Girl," was recently featured by the Saturday Evening Post. The day before she took her life, Miss French penned a remarkable short poem, "Ave atque Vale," in which she sounds the note of tragedy and clearly indicates a state of mind which may account for her last fatal act of self-destruction.

NEWS COMES BY TELEGRAM

The first intimation that reached this city of the suicide of Miss French was contained in a telegram which Poet George Sterling received from his wife yesterday morning in this city. The dispatch was brief and merely recited the fact that Miss French had taken her life. Sterling immediately left for his bungalow at Carmel-by-the-Sea, on the shores of Monterey bay. He was accompanied by Harry A. Lafler, whom he advised of the death of Miss French.

For several weeks Miss French has been the guest of Mrs. Sterling at Carmel. It was the intention of the poetess to leave within a few days for Los Angeles where her father and sister, Miss H. A. French, reside, at 1537

Cambria Street. She had advised friends here that she was going to the southern city and did not know when she would return to San Francisco.

Mrs. Sterling and Miss French were the only occupants of the Sterling bungalow, and retired as usual about midnight. At that time, according to Mrs. Sterling, the young poetess appeared to be in her usual spirits and no concern was entertained by the elder lady concerning her guest. Toward morning Mrs. Sterling heard Miss French rise, and calling to her she received a reassuring reply. She declares that she then heard Miss French lie down again. A moment later the strange breathing of the young woman aroused Mrs. Sterling's fears. She lighted a lamp and found the poetess was dying. Mrs. Sterling ran for assistance, and although Dr. Beck arrived on the scene a short time afterward, his coming was too late and medical aid was of no avail.

TOOK CYANIDE OF POTASSIUM

Coroner Muller of Monterey county held an inquest during the afternoon and the jury returned a verdict of suicide. It was found that on Wednesday morning Miss French had bought a quantity of cyanide of potassium from Dr. Beck, who is also a pharmacist at Monterey, for the alleged purpose of cleaning some silverware. The Coroner stated that the evidences of cyanide poisoning were unmistakable. It is believed that Miss French swallowed the lethal draught while Mrs. Sterling was sleeping. Death ensued almost immediately, and the unfortunate woman died in great physical agony. Miss French is survived by her father and sister, who were advised of the sad news of her death by telegraph, and they immediately left Los Angeles for Carmel-by-the-Sea to take charge of the remains. The young poetess was loved and respected by a host of friends in this city and her passing will be mourned as a calamity in literary circles. The muse of the dead poetess was melancholy and pensive always. Sometimes there was a tinge of morbidness in her writings. One of her most attractive bits of verse, entitled "The Mirage," is full of vain, exquisite longing and sadness. It follows:

["Mirage," quoted in full, the same as in *Poems*.]

[The above article begins on the front page and continues on an inner one. To the right of the article on the front page is a portrait but sketched from a different photograph by Arnold Genthe than the one used as the frontispiece for *Poems*. Above the portrait the caption reads:

Nora May French, whose suicide in the bungalow of Poet George Sterling at Carmel-by-the-Sea has proved a horrifying shock to the local colony of artists and writers.

Sketched by Del Mue from a photo by Genthe.

Below the portrait the poem "Ave atque Vale" is featured, quoted in full, and above the poem the caption incorrectly states:

The last poem of Nora May French, written the day before she ended her young life at the Sterling bungalow at Carmel-by-the-Sea. The poem throbs with a note of tragedy.

Above the continuation of the article on the inner page reads the following:

NORA MAY FRENCH ENDS HER LIFE
Bohemian Circles Shocked by Suicide of Young Poet at Carmel.

The version of "Ave atque Vale" is almost exactly the same as in *Poems*.]

San Francisco Examiner, Friday, November 15, 1907.

MIDNIGHT LURE OF DEATH LEADS POETESS TO GRAVE
Nora M. French Drinks Acid in Poet's Home
Dies in Few Minutes as Mrs. George Sterling
Frantically Chafes Cold Hands
Had Beauty, Suitors, Fame, and Many Friends
But Brooded Constantly over Ill Health—Sister is Prostrated

Actors in the Tragedy of a Poetess
Nora May French, writer of verse
Mrs. George Sterling, wife of author of "A Wine of Wizardry"
James Hopper, author
Fred Bechdolt, author
Dr. Beck, who sold poetess cyanide of potassium
Uncle of Poetess, minister with a suicide theory
Scene—George Sterling's bungalow at Carmel-by-the-Sea
Time—Midnight

Awaiting the coming of Death as a maiden listeneth for the footfall of her lover, Nora May French, loveliest of women, yielded her young life to the grim specter's chill embrace Wednesday night in the home of Mr. and Mrs. George Sterling on the sands of Carmel-by-the-Sea.

Strange tryst with Death! Strange beyond belief that one so beautiful, so talented, so beloved by men and women, should turn from the warm sunlight of success and her own radiant reflection in the mirror waters of the bay near the whispering pines, to the darkness of the Unknown Land!

It was of her that George Sterling once said: "She writes the best sonnets of any young writer that I know."

At the final stroke of midnight Nora May French put poison to her beautiful lips—lips that in all reason should have had the happy seal of love and marriage placed upon them by someone chosen from her many admirers—and in a moment was herself [one] "with yesterday's ten thousand years."

Cyanide of potassium was the means to this sad end. So passed her soul, winging its way from the wooded shore where seeming the most lightsome of her hours had been spent.

Every blessing was hers, save the one priceless possession of perfect health. What impelled her to destroy herself, who can say with certainty? She left no message in that last hour. She made no sign.

Miss French was a Los Angeles girl, her father being an officer of the Old Soldier's Home near Santa Monica. She came to San Francisco soon after the fire and lived with her sister Helen on Lombard Street.

Here her beauty won every eye, and her special literary ability and attainments won an instant place in the literary colony. She was twenty-six years of age, tall, graceful, naturally blonde, with a wealth of tawny hair and deep blue eyes that had poetry in their every glance.

She loved the lighter side of life, with a touch of higher Bohemianism, and the literary work had such a charm for her that she devoted herself to it with an entire absorption. She wrote much poetry, though she was modest about her powers and published little. Her sonnets became known to the few, but rarely could she be persuaded to let the world have a peep at them.

Her prose was strong and sentient, and she balked at no fatigue to secure material for her tales. Thinking there was a chance for fame in the tale of the work of a telephone girl, she secured a place in one of the big exchanges here and toiled for weeks with the "hello girls" in order to steep herself in local color.

Her manuscript on this was accepted and published by the "Saturday Evening Post" of Philadelphia, and the wider literary world began to notice her and predict her fame.

In the October "Sunset" was printed the following sonnet from her pen that seems to presage her disappointment and dissatisfaction with life. It was entitled "Mirage."

[The article quotes in full the sonnet in question, the same as in its appearance in *Poems*.]

Some little time ago the stately young beauty felt that her health was failing and that she needed a change. Her sister went to Los Angeles and she found a congenial home with Mr. and Mrs. George Sterling at Carmel-by-the-Sea. There the Sterlings have a charming home just at the edge of the pines, with an outlook upon the wondrous valley of the Carmel mission.

In this atmosphere of balsamic aromas and sea breezes her health rapidly improved and her natural robustness seemed about to return. She found also a congenial literary atmosphere, as there is the nucleus of a fine literary and artistic colony at Carmel and across the hills at Monterey. Her constant associates were the Sterlings, Mary Austin, Mr. and Mrs. James Hopper and the others of their brilliant coterie; while Charles Rollo Peters, Charles Dickman, Charles Stuart Fonda and the other artists made frequent visits for picnics or al fresco reunions.

Miss French roamed at will. Dressed in khaki, with short skirt, high boots and her blonde head rumpled by the breeze, she made a picture as she walked the woodland paths or wandered along the sand—a picture to linger in the eye and to be brought up by memory in the after years. It was supposed that she was engaged to be married to a stalwart Englishman, while a young writer of the ultra Bohemian set in San Francisco was said to be eating his disappointed heart out for her.

Her work was sought for by the magazines and higher class publications, and there seemed everything for her to live for—returned health, increasing fame, advantageous matrimony, general admiration. And yet she chose to put the poison to her lips and die without a sign.

It seems she brooded on death and the sudden dispatch. Her poetic temperament and high strung nervous nature took to the contemplation of the grave as most young women contemplate social success or matrimonial favor. Her life was in a world of romance, but her favored suitor always seemed to wear the mysterious veil under which the death's head leered.

An uncle of Miss French, a Presbyterian minister of a temperament very like her own, talked with her of suicide—talked calmly and philosophically, as if self-destruction were a possibly excusable end for earthly disappointments, and he said to her grimly: "Whenever you feel like committing suicide sit down near an approaching shadow and say to yourself that as soon as the shadow reaches you, you will kill yourself. Then when the shadow reaches you, put the revolver to your head and shoot. That will cure you."

On Monday last the handsome woman had this advice of the grim old Presbyterian full in her mind. She was reading one of Housman's poems, in which a Shropshire lad shoots himself with a revolver. She wrote under one line: "Bravely done, my lad; bravely done!"

Then she fetched George Sterling's revolver and went out into a lonely place, where the shadows were her only companions. She picked one shadow as she sat down, and she said to herself, after her stern philosophical uncle's advice: "When that shadow reaches me I will kill myself!"

On came the shadow—on and on and on. The fine girl braced herself for its approach as for the approach of a lover. She lifted the revolver to her head. The shadow neared, and she fired. But her nerve faltered at the last minute. She shot away just one golden curl from her fair head, and the breeze played pranks with the bit of hair that lovers would have fought over. She picked up the hair and returned to the house. Mrs. Sterling had seen the underscoring in Housman's book and had missed her husband's revolver. She was deep in fear and apprehension when Nora May French came tripping in, bearing the curl in triumph. That night she told Mrs. Sterling how she had intended death and made all her preparations, and then how she couldn't bear the shock of the rude bullet in her brain.

But with this episode she declared she was cured of her desires for death, and her demeanor was happy and natural. She continued her daily round of freedom, with walks and communions varied by a dip in the sea. And still every eye followed her in admiration and perhaps in envy at her happiness and beauty.

The canker was in her soul, however, and on Wednesday morning she went to the home of Dr. Beck and got some cyanide of potassium—quickest and most certain of poisons. With it death comes in a breath. No call is more sudden. Nothing is further beyond the reach of antidotes. She secured the acid by saying she wished to use it for polishing silver.

She had studied the poison, knew just what the acid could be used for in the peaceful arts, and just how to make of it a lethal draught. That day and night she was alone at the Sterling home with Mrs. Sterling, the head of the house having been called to Oakland on business. And this is how Mrs. Sterling yesterday told the story of the tragedy—tells it in her forthright way without effort at effect or dramaturgy:

"Nora May and I retired early last night, about 10 o'clock, and Nora May seemed to be in a most cheerful mood. We slept in the same room in separate beds. Between the beds was a small table. I was awakened by the creaking of the bathroom door just as the clock was striking midnight.

"I called out, 'Is that you, Nora May?' She answered, 'Yes, I want a drink of water.'

"I heard her pour a glass of water and then return to the room and lie down on the bed. A few seconds after, I heard a strange catching noise in her throat. I lit a match.

"Nora May lay back on the bed stiff. There was foam at her lips. I thought she had hysterics. I said, 'Now you be good, Nora May.'

"The foam went away, the catching noise stopped, her face became normal and then pale. I thought she was getting better. I put wet towels around her head. I sat on the edge of the bed until I became chilled.

"Then finding her cold, I got into the bed beside her to warm her. While lying there trying to warm her I saw on the table a glass at the bottom of which was a white powder sediment.

"I ran out of the room and looked up a medical book in the library. Mary Austin, the author, is writing a book in which the heroine kills herself with cyanide of potassium, and I remembered that Nora asked all about the effects of cyanide of potassium, and I looked for an antidote. Then I became frightened and ran across the stretch of woods and the sand dunes to the home of James Hopper and Fred Bechdolt, the writers."

Hopper and Bechdolt are collaborating and live together in a cottage. Both got out of bed when Mrs. Sterling knocked, and while Hopper went for Dr. Beck, Bechdolt went to the Sterling home with Mrs. Sterling. When Hopper and Dr. Beck arrived it was found the beautiful and gifted girl was dead and had been within a few seconds after she returned from the bathroom. The poison had struck at her heart on the instant.

The party spent the night telegraphing friends and relatives. At 11 o'clock Coroner Muller arrived, impaneled a jury and heard the evidence of Mrs. Sterling, Hopper and Bechdolt. As Mrs. Sterling testified the jury wept. No sadder tale had ever been told in the pretty village in the pines by the sea.

"'Killed by poetry' is what you might put on her tombstone," said one of her friends in discussing her case. "She lived in a realm of poesy and the unreal, and death always seemed to have as much charm for her as life. Yet she was capable of the sanest efforts when she chose, as everyone can see by reading her 'Diary of a Telephone Girl,' for which she worked so long and so hard.

"But she was given to silences and self-communings. She would go out to the sand dunes at Point Lobos and sit by the hour studying the sea. Her poem

'Mirage' was the result of one of these afternoons with the sand and the ocean. Then she would jump on a horse and dash for long and lonely rides, returning with a poem which she would read to friends and then throw away.

"Hers were strange ways, but she was one of the most naturally beautiful women I ever saw. Her age was 26 and she was just in the full flush of her beauty. In figure she was taller than most women, but graceful and rounded. Her eyes were of the sea blue, and her complexion of the most delicate pink and white, but her brows were dark as night, and the combination gave her the rare beauty that so many women attempt with artificial aid.

"And she had what is rare in women—humor and a sense of it. But even that did not save her from the clutch of melancholy veiled by a seemingly happy exterior. Her success and the promise of fame did not satisfy her. Love of men was not enough. Death was to her the only happiness."

San Francisco society was to have seen and heard her on Thanksgiving eve, when she was to have read at the Fairmont. But instead of the applause and compliments of society she preferred the grave and the great poetic silences.

[The article ends with a quotation in full of "Ave atque Vale," stating incorrectly that it was her last poem. The article begins on the front page and continues on an inner one. Amid the artwork signed by V. Nahl—which precedes the article, and which includes a portrait sketched from the photograph by Arnold Genthe, the same used as the frontispiece for *Poems*—the sonnet "Between Two Rains" is quoted in full.]

Los Angeles Times, Friday, November 15, 1907.

BY HER OWN HAND.
YOUNG WOMAN ENDS HER LIFE.
RISES AT MIDNIGHT HOUR AND TAKES POISON.

Young and Beautiful Woman Who
Has Written Verse for Magazines
Carries Out Suicidal Impulse Long
Entertained—Father and Sister
Residents of Los Angeles.

[BY DIRECT WIRE TO THE TIMES.]

MONTEREY, Nov. 14. —[Exclusive Dispatch.] Nora May French, a young and beautiful woman, who had written some verse for the magazines, took her life this morning at the home of Mrs. George Sterling at Carmel-by-the-Sea, with a draught of potassium cyanide.

The young woman, who was loved and respected by hosts of friends, had long suffered with suicidal impulse. Lately she had made her home with Mrs. Sterling, wife of the well-known poet, George Sterling. The poet has been absent in San Francisco for a few days, and Miss French and Mrs. Sterling were the only occupants of the Sterling bungalow.

Just after midnight this morning Mrs. Sterling heard Miss French rise, then lie down again. A moment later the strange breathing of the young woman aroused the fear of Mrs. Sterling, who lit a lamp and found Miss French dying. Mrs. Sterling ran out for assistance. This was promptly given, but too late.

Coroner Muller held an inquest this afternoon, and the jury gave a verdict of suicide. It was found that Miss French on Wednesday morning had bought from Dr. Beck a large amount of cyanide of potassium, under the plea of using it for cleaning silverware. Mrs. Sterling is prostrated by the affair.

Miss French's father and sister, Helen, are living in Los Angeles. Since shortly after the earthquake and up to the time, two weeks ago, when she took up her home with the Sterlings, Miss French had been living in San Francisco. Her sister two weeks ago returned to Los Angeles. Her father and sister have been telegraphed for.

[The "two weeks" mentioned twice in the last paragraph above should of course be "two months."]

Los Angeles Times, Sunday, November 17, 1907.

Pacific Slope.

CAST ASHES ON SEA SHE LOVED.

*Family and Friends of Poet Perform Rites Today.
Body of Nora May French Is Cremated in North.
Salem [sic] Ceremony Takes Place at Cypress Point.*

[BY DIRECT WIRE TO THE TIMES.]

16 SAN FRANCISCO, Nov. 16.—[Exclusive Dispatch.] Tomorrow at the famous Cypress Point, on the seventeen-mile drive at historic Monterey, the ashes of Nora May French, the young Los Angeles poet, who took her own life

last Thursday, will be scattered on the ocean. The body was cremated here today and the ashes will be taken down to Monterey by the morning train.

Her father and her sister, Miss Helen French, George Sterling, the poet, and his wife, Jimmie Hopper and his wife, Mrs. Mary Austin and other intimate friends of the deceased will gather at Cypress Point and cast the ashes into the waves that beat upon the promontory. The shade of the old oak there, the favorite of painters and poets, was one of her places for contemplation.

During the two weeks [i.e., two months] that she lived at Carmel-by-the-Sea, she often rode to the point, and, resting there, brooded for hours at a time—and no doubt worked out at that place the details of the act that gave sorrow to her friends and robbed the world of a talented woman.

Those who knew her best will gather at old Cypress tomorrow and there will be little ceremony and no ostentation about the giving of her ashes to the ocean. Short and simple rites will mark the act which is to make her part of the sea and the shore by which she sat and planned this consummation.

The facts have come out that she suffered from an organic disease and that, though she was engaged to marry Capt. Thomas Allan Haley [sic], an Englishman, who fought on the Boer side in the South African war, she was very despondent and feared that her health would prevent her marriage.

Los Angeles Times, Monday, 18 November 1907.

POSTPONE LAST RITES.

Friends of Nora May French Wish to Avoid Publicity in Casting Ashes on Pacific.

[BY DIRECT WIRE TO THE TIMES.]

MONTEREY, November 17. —[Exclusive Dispatch.] The scattering on the Pacific of the ashes of Nora May French has been postponed by the friends of the dead poetess. No date has been assigned for the ceremony.

It is evident that the friends wish to avoid publicity and to have present only those who really cared for the dead girl.

Town Talk, (Saturday,) 23 November 1907.
Department "The Spectator" (probably by the editor, Theodore F. Bonnet)

A HOPELESS SINGER

If we knew the whole truth behind the recent tragedy at Carmel-by-the-Sea it might be commonplace enough. Suicide is one of the ordinary methods of avoiding the annoyance of what we call existence. Those who traverse this by-path to the Dark Beyond are usually a little weaker, a little less sanguine of the eternal fitness of things than are their fellow travelers on the high road from the cradle to the tomb. Sometimes we of coarser fiber think that the impatient one was unbalanced mentally, but until we agree upon a standard of sanity we may not say that one who violently anticipates the inevitable is abnormal. Most of us, by extending the area of motive for suicide, can easily call to mind instances of an insane desire to live, when in fact, it would be absolute proof of returning reason if the one so possessed with the life mania would begin to realize the helplessness and the hopelessness of his living condition and finally, with sincere approval of his highest faculties and his purest emotions, end it all swiftly and irretrievably. The Carmel suicide was a poet. Her disposition was to look upon life as through a glass, darkly. She brooded upon imaginary sorrows as is the habit of poets whose poetry lives in the hearts of men. Her skies were leaden and gray; her sunlight was merely "a silver space between two rains"; the songs of the birds were dirges and requiems in memory of the dead leaves; she "wandered silent through the waning land," and the "old, old lichen crumbled in her hand"; she groped through "strange mists," and her hands were always "giving greeting and farewell," in "empty plains where hot horizons swim,"—a greeting to something indefinite, vague and unattainable; a farewell to something that inspired love in "a mood too sweet for tears, for joy too pale." So she wrote her thoughts in words, but never a hint of hope, of worldly aspiration, of confidence in the purpose of her being.

PESSIMISM WITHOUT DESPAIR

This on the pallid surface of the tragedy at Carmel. What may have lurked beneath we may not know and it would be presumptuous impertinence to inquire; for a dead woman's secrets are as sacred as her memory. Apparently, however, this young woman from constant brooding upon the hopelessness and uncertainty of it all, had hypnotized herself into the belief that life was not worth living. She began, no doubt, with the idea that the sweetest songs are those that are sung in the minor key; and gradually she came to hear dirges and requiems in the songs of the birds and threnodies in the low sighing winds and the lapping of the waves on the seashore, while "seaward fared again with litten sail [/] her laden ship of dreams adown the sky." This was not the mood of Keats or Shelley or Tennyson, and it was far from the mood of Wordsworth; these sang many of their songs in the minor key, but they were not morbid in the singing; they sang of death and decay and the passing of things mortal, but there was a hopeful lilt in their tone and a purpose to make the best of what was given in the parceling of good and evil to men and women; they sang as the linnet sings in the ticket, sadly, sweetly, but resolutely for the joy of singing—not with the egotism of despair nor as the swan sings because he welcomes death.

Current Literature, June 1908.
Department "Recent Poetry."

It may seem a little late to be reprinting a poem on the San Francisco fire, written and published shortly after that event; but the sad death of the author, by her own hand, a few months ago, lends a new and melancholy interest to the fine stanzas below, and having missed the poem at the time it first appeared in the San Francisco *Call*, we take this opportunity to atone for the omission. Miss French was a resident of Los Angeles, a frail girl of twenty-four, when she ended her promising career, at Carmel, in the bungalow of George Sterling, the poet, being at the time the guest of Mr. Sterling and his wife.

["Says the Old Year to the New," quoted in full, the same as "San Francisco, New Year's, 1906," with slight differences.]

San Francisco Call, Sunday, 12 June 1910.
Department "Book Page of the Call," conducted by Una H. H. Cool, from "Brief Reviews of New Books."

(Accompanied by the now standard portrait by Arnold Genthe preceding the title page in *Poems*).

The poems of the late Nora May French, whose tragic death at Carmel in 1907 cast a gloom over the literary colony of the west, have been collected and edited by Henry Anderson Lafler, assisted by Porter Garnett and George Sterling. There are more than it was generally supposed Miss French had written, and some are of great beauty. Most of them have seen publication before, but a few included in this collection which have never been printed. The book is daintily printed and bound. (The Strange Company, San Francisco.)

[The following article from the *New Age* remains the only known full review of Nora May French's *Poems* that has emerged, apart from the later article that appeared in Holland in late 1910. The periodical itself was published in London, curiously enough. The trio producing *Poems*—Garnett, Lafler, and Sterling, with possible financial assistance from Jack London—evidently sent out few copies for review, and so we find few regular reviews of it in any of the Bay Area newspapers, including the four San Francisco papers, the *Bulletin*, the *Call*, the *Chronicle*, and the *Examiner*, or such periodicals as *Town Talk*, the *Argonaut*, and the *Overland Monthly*, with the one exception of the *Call*. A careful search through these publications for June and July 1910, in the regular book-reviewing departments or columns, reveals only one direct mention of the book. In the newspapers in question the regular reviews usually appear on Sunday, or less often on Saturday. Possibly the dismissive and uncomprehending reaction to Nora May's poetry and suicide by editor Theodore F. Bonnet in the issue of *Town Talk* for 23 November 1907 dissuaded the trio from wasting copies on potentially opaque journalists. The strategy worked, and the small edition sold out rapidly, buoyed up only by word of mouth among Northern California's Bohemian community. Bonnet's remark, that Nora May as a poet sang "with the egotism of despair," must have rankled the people forming the Strange Company. For once, or so it might appear, the quality of the volume and its successful sale represented the triumph of the artists themselves, united on behalf of a fallen comrade, vis-à-vis the ambient non-artists, however sympathetic otherwise.]

The New Age: A Weekly Review of Politics, Literature and Art,
Thursday, 14 July 1910.

A Book of Beauty
Michael Williams

The *Poems* of Nora May French have been collected and published (The Strange Company, San Francisco). Ninety slim pages suffice to hold all the work that the editor of the little volume deemed worthy to represent the young, beautiful girl who killed herself in Carmel, California, three years ago. But nearly every line of these poems achieves the aim of poetry—which is, Beauty. Hence, in a time like this, when the printing press spews forth countless objects of no account, true ineptitudes, together with many poisonous and evil things, but so rarely gives birth to real objects of true art, the appearance of this little book of naive—yet art-created—beauty is a matter of importance to all those who care for poetry and are concerned regarding America's contributions to the greatest of the arts.

Nora May French was twenty-six years old when she drank poison and died, leaving directions that her body be burned and the ashes cast into the sea from the granite cliffs of Point Lobos. This is not the occasion to study the sad history of a temperament that could not achieve harmony with its environment; more than to say that her temperament was poetic in excelsis, and her environment constituted of Mammon's worse conditions. Poverty and sickness, and ever-baffled yearnings for a life of romance and beauty impossible for her to live, at last brought this victim of a horrible civilization to her knees in "the outer court" of death. She wrote a distinctly prophetic sonnet a year and four months before she died:

["The Outer Gate," quoted in full.]

This young girl—for even at twenty-six she was still in some respects a child, and many of her poems were written years before her death—this young girl had at her command a creative magic of a poignantly beautiful and haunting quality; a magic for which the only word seems to be "spiritual." For while the allure and beauty of material things were always near and dear, yet something concealed for most people within the outward semblances ever thrilled her most sensitive apprehension of inner things—of the spirit and the soul. Yet, unhappily, it was the inner appeal, and the haunting soul, of sadness, of hopelessness (for all souls are not happy and satisfied and good), that ever weighed upon Nora May French.

She lay so unguarded and open to spiritual impressions that at times it would almost seem as if the spiritual world had become objectified to her. In dreams, at least ("dreams" is the word by which we speak of a life impossible to speak of intelligibly), she must have had singular adventures; for here are some prose words which she brought back in memory from a dream:—

["Think Not, O Lilias," quoted in full.]

The soul of this wonderful girl—who was obliged to earn her bread for a period by the flesh-and-nerve-destroying toil of a "hello girl" at a telephone exchange switchboard—had a magical gift of transmuting impressions from the ethereal vibrations of Nature's finer forces, as manifested in beautiful land-and-sea-and-sky-scapes especially, that gives to her poetry a quality most exquisite and memorable—memorable, not as rhetoric is, memorable, in static phrases, but memorable rather as music is memorable: in haunting cadences and evocations of an atmosphere of mystical suggestions—suggestions of beauty, of sorrow, and pain; with occasional radiations of a pure lyrical joy.

["Yesterday," quoted in full.]

The chief "work" contained in the little book is "The Spanish Girl," a love tale told in separate poems of uneven quality; some of them are perfect. A strong and subtle sense of passion throbs in this lyric sequence. To quote accurately were to copy all, or nearly all.

But I cannot forbear to copy the sonnet, written for a friend on the occasion of his marriage, entitled, rather too vaguely, "The Rose":—

["The Rose," quoted in part.]

The editor of the book—Mr. Henry Anderson Lafler, who was aided by Mr. George Sterling and Mr. Porter Garnett—has well achieved his part, for the volume is excellently printed and the verses arranged with pleasing art, while the notes are simply those called for to explain a few points in the text.

Oh, little book of beauty!—vibrant message from one lonely woman's inmost heart—may you find your way to beauty's friends in the world!

[Although it might seem curious that the only known full review of Nora May's *Poems* (apart form the later article published in Holland late in 1910)—and it certainly ranks as criticism of an elevated kind—should have appeared in a weekly magazine published in London; it is a fact that from the 1870s into the 1920s and even 1930s, Californian literary figures and their works enjoyed a greater réclame in London than they did in New York City thanks to the literary beachhead established in Britain in the 1870s by such Californian writers as the poet Joaquin Miller and the satirist Ambrose Bierce. Miller sojourned and cut a flamboyant figure there as a carefully calculated Wild West character, and Bierce worked and lived there for several years in the same way as Miller. Michael Williams himself was a Californian writer who wrote for the San Francisco press *inter alia*.]

Current Literature, September 1910.
Department "Recent Poetry."

The tragic history of the author lends additional interest to the poems of Norah May French, gathered by her sister for the Strange Company, San Francisco. Poverty and disease pursued this delicate girl; at one time she was forced to earn her living as telephone operator. At length, unable to stand the stress of daily life, Miss French sought death by her own hand. "Nearly every line of her poetry," remarks *The New Age* (London), "achieves the aim of poetry which is Beauty. Hence, in a time like this, when the printing press spews forth countless objects of no account, true ineptitudes, together with many poisonous and evil things, but so rarely gives birth to real objects of true art, the appearance of this little book of naive—yet art-created—beauty is a matter of importance to all those who care for poetry and are concerned regarding America's contributions to the greatest of the arts."

["Yesterday," by Norah May French, quoted in full.]

[Apart from the notice in the San Francisco *Call* and the article in *De Nieuwe Gids*, this appears to be the only American notice for the *Poems* of 1910 at the time, and it is significant that this East-Coast periodical evidently noted it from the review in the *New Age* published in Great Britain.]

Die Nieuwe Gids [The New Guidebook], November 1910.

From the Lands Overseas
Hein Boeken.

In Memory of Nora May French,
born at Aurora [New York], April 1881,
died at Carmel in California 14 Nov. 1907.

Because my love has wave and foam for speech,
    And never words, and yearns as water grieves,
With white arms curving on a listless beach,
    And murmurs inarticulate as leaves—

I am become beloved of the night—
    Her huge sea-lands ineffable and far

> Hold crouched and splendid Sorrow eyed with light,
> And Pain who beads his forehead with a star.
> ["The Mourner" by Nora May French]

All of you rise with me now, those few likeminded solitary people, if there are any of you at all, and follow with me the sun's glorious daily path over the sea—hear its great voice—and come to the place that carries its name to the Dawn, because it is in that land where the sun rises from the sea, that you can behold the sun for the first time.

Go over there, following the path over the waves during the night, because then you will see in that place, together with the sun, its emerging waves reflected. And your ears, which drank silence above the Great One, the ever-moving one that lets its voice be heard first when it approaches the peopled shores—your ears will be susceptible to the tones there that I want you to hear.

For if he who has had the voices of many people in his ears, as they speak in their everyday language about winning and losing, about greed and gluttony, to him those tones do not convey the soul's language that they carry with them.

Only a few people live there in that place, and they quietly and silently repeat—from time to time—the words that the One [i.e., Nora May French] spoke there, spoke here and in few other places where she lived later on. And they repeat those words because they lingered in their minds, carried on the wings of [poetic] rhythm. And they see them and must keep seeing them, those faces, because an incandescent eye has forced them to see them along with her.

When she was a child no longer or was barely still a child, she had to toil in life just like other people, who had no other hunger or thirst than the hunger and thirst for food and drink—because she too had to provide for the hunger and thirst of her body. But more than her body's toiling and suffering, she had her own [poetic] labor, from heavenly delight down to hellish pain—this gave her no peace, even though her physical labor had been accomplished. And this arose during the incandescent nights, but remained with her on into the somber or cold-lit day.

Like the voice of the great Sea, which brought the sun to her and over which the awesome star-studded Night arose, the comforting Mother in eternal mourning, thus and even more intense and undulant and throbbing was the heaving in her own chest.

And like the sun, which the sea brought to her daily, thus a sun would dawn for her from a human being—there were so many people who looked upon her, and whose looks and eyes promised suns or distant shimmering nights. But still it was not the one for whom she was waiting. But he would appear, she knew that. She was assured of that.

And that sun she would follow like the processions of people, which she saw daily coming over the sea, and which she saw pursuing their own sun over the lands and plains into the mountains, and on into diversified, appropriate and vigorous life and labor in the founding of cities and the settlement of people.

But that sun—it challenged her—had it faded or hidden itself behind clouds?

And the loud and humid house, which life had bestowed on her, oppressed her more and more, that her life, that rich life that seemed to offer everything to her, seemed to withhold everything from her as well. Loud were the assembled and roaring voices, to her the taunting voices—oh sometimes loud with yearning, joyous music—sultry with desires and needs—but that house had only one exit, through which a cool breeze was blowing inside. . . .

Oh her soul that she searched, with how many threads was it attached to the invisible, the untraceable. . . .

Oh this life, if she ever left it, would there be another life that would offer her lavishly what this life had withheld from her? This life, so rich in temptations, deluded with false hopes, so impoverished in its. . . . Would that other life offer her what this one withheld from her so tauntingly?

But louder and louder grew the voice of the Sea, out of which the great Night arose.

So that the Sea and the Night now possess her—her body rests in the earth—but above the Sea during the Night, where the great Desires live in peace, above the Sea, which remains silent but which at first has a voice that can lure and disturb people, as they hear its voice augment and echo among the rocks and the beaches. There she is in the great Eternal Desires, which turn into flesh and into unavoidable battles, but which ultimately receive in eternal peace those who suffered this life—oh miserable mortal—in lifelong discontentment.

Poems by Nora May French, San Francisco, the Strange Company, 1910.
Hilversum, 24 Sept. 1910.

GOD AND SATYR

By HEIN BOEKEN

A MYTHICAL POLEMIC

Shall I view Apollo? Thus I asked, then I viewed him—
   Or was it fancy or illusion, which he sent
   To test him whom he found to be his worthy peer?
It seemed just fine, because had not the day pursued him

Flat on the vessel's planks? Did not the throb escort him
   That issued from the loud and thunder-rolling waves,
   Removing him far from the Father's love supreme?
But, woe is him! why did the Satyr's laugh desert him?

Or am I more, myself, of Bacchical descent
   Because I am drawn more to chirp and trill of bird,
      And thus drawn more to Nature's voices infinite

Than—was it something more than lovely sounds alone
   Rather than breath and flash of changeable word-play
      Of which he boasts with Culture unbeknown by me?

[Hilversum lies about ten miles southeast of Amsterdam. Dr. Marcel van Baal (professor of linguistics), of Tujunga, California, has graciously supplied the translation of this article from which Donald Sidney-Fryer has rehandled the English so as to make it rather more coherent. It is difficult to determine how to classify this article: it is not a regular review, if review at all, unless we use the term "impressionistic reverie," insightfully furnished by poet and critic Marvin R. Hiemstra, of San Francisco, who first examined the piece for us in Dutch. How paradoxical that the poetry of Nora May French, remarkable for its classically limpid but still profound character, should have inspired what seems in the original Dutch to be such a difficult, and rather involuted, poetic prose! Incidentally, the ellipses are Boeken's own and not the editors'.

We have also included the sonnet "God and Satyr" by Hein Boeken (again graciously given us in a translation by Dr. van Baal), which immediately follows his article, on the assumption that he may have intended it in some subtle manner as a kind of supplement or companion piece. There are some direct links—such as the sea, the sun, the song of birds, and the infinite voices of Nature—which connote with the same in the poetry of Nora May French. Again Donald Sidney-Fryer has rehandled the English of Boeken's poem.]

Poems by Nora May French, The California Literary Pamphlets, Number 2: The Book Club of California, 1936.
"Foreword" by Sara Bard Field.

Of Nora May French's poetry George Sterling, her distinguished contemporary, said, "Whenever she put her pen to paper something perfect was the result." It is that quality of consistent if imponderable loveliness that makes the poetry of this California poet worthy of re-attention.

Born in 1881, Nora's brief life-span touched that of Emily Dickinson in time by five years. To press a comparison between the two poets would be unfair, Emily Dickinson, a great original, living more than twice as long as Nora May French, saw her work gain volume and maturity. Nora May French, a trifle older than Keats and three years younger than Shelley at the time of her death, left only a slender volume of fifty-three lyrical poems, if we treat the twenty-two poems of *The Spanish Girl* as one. Her forms are traditional, her thinking neither so breathless in content nor so daring in expression as Emily's. For that matter what other poet's is? She is persuasive rather than startling. Her poetic ultimate is accomplished by a caress rather than a shock. She never achieved the Blake-like brevity of Emily's "stenographic messages from heaven" nor ever ascended the dizzy metaphysical heights of the elder poet. Nevertheless she is metaphysical and for the most part brief. Emily Dickinson might have written such lines as Nora May French's poem "Vivisection" or such lines as

> My eyes are level with the grass
> And up and down each slender steep
> I watch the tiny people pass.
> or
> I tilt my hollowed life and look within
> or
> I lay my joy within this hollowed space.

Both these poets opened wide arms to Nature, both poured all of heart and mind into the making of any poem. Death, too, beckoned each of them. For Emily, Death was a vast white mystery to be examined with delicate, unwearied fingers; for Nora, a siren call, an alluring experience to be realized at the sacrifice of all that Life offered. Emily was content to await it. Nora rushed toward it, ending her life at the age of twenty-six.

California's claim to this poet is unchallenged. Though born in Aurora, New York, she lived twenty years of her brief life in this state. Most people pass or spend their lives in places. Their citizenship is a matter of arithmetic and external facts. Hers was a matter of profoundly feeling and absorbing California. Her devotion has not left its record in the dark thunder of Robinson Jeffers. The sea beats against her verses insistently but with quiet sadness. In and out of her lines California steps and resteps—its manzanita thickets, its orange groves, its Spanish Missions, its olive slopes, its poppy fields—the streets, docks, and bay of San Francisco. Here is a typical scene, familiar to all Californians pictured with swift charm.

> The manzanita stirs!
> Look, in that little thicket just ahead!
> Down, down, the covey whirrs,
> Mocking us, careful, led,
> Slow-slipping beads along a slender thread.

The Spanish Girl, a lyrical sequence of twenty-two poems, in three parts, is Nora May French's most considerable work. In these lyrics, the color, the atmosphere, the lightly suggested historical background of the state are woven into a work deserving a special brochure. There remains space for only passing comment on one of the miracles of art—the emergence of a personality from this handful of poems: a sensitive, tender woman feeling the world through delicate antennae of over-sensitive nerves, obsessed with Beauty, haunted by some unattainable Ideal, pitiful of human pain and the sorrow of dumb creatures, dazzled by color but compelled by shadow, knowing love as twin but opposing ecstasies, believing in Life but unable to resist Death. Had she done so, I believe her work might have ripened with the years. Its loveliness, now fragile, might have gained bone and—sinew and stature. Her measure, inclining to monotony, might have acquired a various tone, a more subtle rhythm, a profounder sweep. She knew of what elements poetry is composed. She might have taken her place among America's foremost women poets. Even her thin note is haunting as the hermit thrush's and as sweet. Though she sits back in the "verdurous gloom" where her voice is drowned when the oriole or nightingale sings, she will keep her humble hold on the poetic bough.

[NORA MAY FRENCH AND THE QUESTION OF MATURITY

According to Michael Williams in his rare extant review devoted to *Poems* and its author, as published in the *New Age* for 14 July 1910, "Even at twenty-six she was still in some respects a child." In addition, according to Richard Hughey in his empathic preface to his pamphlet reprinting "The Spanish Girl" and other works in July 2003, "She never matured psychologically." These assertions are open to question. From the latter 1890s, when she was seventeen or so, until 1906, when she was twenty-five, she worked when she was not attending school. In particular, from 1898 until 1906, she worked steadily at the carved-leather factory in Los Angeles, designing the pictorial representations realized on and in the leather products manufactured by the factory, apart from the one year in art schools in New York City, 1899–1900, which she considered the happiest period in her life. When the failing finances of her family demanded it, she and her siblings had to go to work, and they did the best that they could without fuss or complaint. Sometime after the family moved from Glendale to Los Angeles, around 1901, the two older brothers had moved out of the household to pursue their own lives and careers by 1905; the mother, Mary Wells French, had become seriously ill, and the father with the daughters nursed the mother through a painful and protracted illness until her demise in July 1905, when the daughters found themselves at home away from their needed employment.

After his wife's death the household broke up, Edward French went to the Old Soldiers' Home in Westwood (near the northeastern corner of Santa Monica), and the girls moved into their own apartment in Los Angeles, thus living together and paying off the family's bills, especially those incurred by the mother's illness. Curiously, reflecting the information vouchsafed by Helen French Hunt, Judith Allen's M.A. thesis on the life and writing of Nora May French makes no further mention of the two older brothers, nor of their helping to pay off their family's indebtedness. A special point: We must not forget that until about World War I children and teenagers became adults de facto more or less in their middle to latter adolescence, that is, when they reached the ability to procreate. Whether on the farm or in the factory, many children went to work as soon as possible, to help the family or to start their own independent existence. Necessity, that stern taskmaster, brought people to some kind of maturation early, fast, and efficiently. Given how she behaved in a responsible manner early in her life, going to work to help support her family or herself, Nora May had ceased being a mere child by middle to late adolescence, thus attaining some kind of maturity perforce much earlier than if her family had not undergone divers financial crises.]

[NORA MAY FRENCH VIS-À-VIS OTHER WOMEN POETS

Although the seventeen pages making up Mary Rudge's incisive and sympathetic introduction to the Star Rover House book of selected poems by Nora May French, published in 1986, are too lengthy to recount here in full, we feel it incumbent on us to quote one of Rudge's most insightful paragraphs, concerning Nora May's rank vis-à-vis other women poets.

> Nora May can be understood best in the context of her time. Her life and works do not need comparison with writers like Anne Sexton, Sylvia Plath, Amy Lowell—the patterns of whose lives were loomed on structures so far removed from that where appeared the brief gold flash of Nora May's genius and colorful life—or of Emily Dickinson, whose time span overlapped Nora May's by a five year period. These had different socio-economic support systems. [. . .]

There in a nutshell Mary Rudge has declared the essential: that Nora May is best understood in the context of her time, even if we can make some fruitful comparisons between her and other women poets past or present. All discussion of their formal brevity and respective metaphysics apart, Sara Bard Field's comparison of Nora May with Emily Dickinson is misleading, because they have really very little in common. Dickinson led a long and relatively quiet existence, free from the need to do mundane jobs to earn her living. Nora May patently did not have that option. Her exceptional beauty, her acute intelligence and literacy, her passionate nature and natural sensuality, the conspicuous attraction that she held for men—all this makes her much closer to someone like Louise Labé (c. 1520–1566), "la Belle Cordière" of Lyon, or like Edna St. Vincent Millay (1892–1950).

This brings us to the closely related question of Nora May vis-à-vis her female friends. Although she stated that she had none and that she inspired nothing but envy from other females, this is not completely true. Of course, Nora May had a good number of special female friends whether in Northern or Southern California: her mother (Mary Wells French), her sister (Helen French Hunt), Mary Austin, Carrie Sterling, Blanche Partington, Ina Coolbrith, and others—but her sister remained her best female friend. Apparently, once women meeting her rose above their initial distrust because of her exceptional beauty, they became very fond of her, devoted to her and her well-being, and somehow realized her essential fragility.]

Helen (Augusta) French Hunt (1883–1973):
A Little Memoir (A Friendship, 1968–1973)

Donald Sidney-Fryer

Her sister Helen was probably Nora May's best and closest friend, and if, when younger, Nora May as the elder of the two looked after Helen, then as young adults the roles reversed, and Helen played elder sister to Nora May as best she could, just as a little later Helen looked after and guarded both Nora May's creative heritage and her personal memory, following the younger sister's death.

It has been my good fortune, over a considerable period of time (roughly 1958 up to the summer of 2006), to have enjoyed both direct and indirect connections to the group of writers and artists now known as the California Romantics, now acknowledged to be as remarkable as that group of English writers and artists who flourished in the early decades of the twentieth century and known collectively as the Bloomsbury Group, named after a section of London where many of them resided. Helen French Hunt, however, emerged as my strongest and most dearly cherished link to the California Romantics, as well as to that increasingly remote period in which they had flourished. In spite of the considerable difference in age between us—she was in her mid-80s and I in my mid-30s when we met—Helen became not only a special friend but, quite unexpectedly, a generous patron and a patient mentor.

Although the brilliant short stories of Clark Ashton Smith served in 1954 as my first introduction to this group, and although I learned of Smith's association with George Sterling as the group's epicenter almost at once, it was not until the spring of 1958—when I first acquired and began to assimilate Smith's first four poetry collections (1912, 1918, 1922, and 1925), three of which remain epochal achievements—that I became conscious of the California Romantics as a group. Subsequently, through the kindly offices of Ethel Heiple (whom I had met at Auburn in September 1957), I made two extended visits with Smith and his wife (the former Carol Jones Dorman), then living in Pacific Grove on the Monterey peninsula, during the latter summers of 1958 and 1959, respectively.

I had already read some of Sterling's poetry, and now Smith himself became a direct personal connection to the elder figure, who had once played mentor to Smith in his own development as a poet. I had first become aware of Nora May French herself in the spring of 1958, when I first read Smith's magnificent memorial poem "To Nora May French" in his second major collection, *Ebony and Crystal* (1922). However, it was not until January 1961, when I was conducting research in the California Section of the California State Library in Sacramento for my Smith bibliography, *Emperor of Dreams* (1978), that I took the opportunity to examine one of the copies in that institution's possession, and to read over, albeit hastily, Nora May French's *Poems* (1910), simply for a quick look-see. Like most people who have had the good fortune to discover this volume, I was arrested not only by the poetry but also by the photo portrait of the poet herself, taken by Arnold Genthe and placed opposite the title page.

Two poems in particular caught my attention, the opening sonnet, "The Outer Gate," and the closing piece, "Ave atque Vale." When I read the third and final stanza of this last poem, I seemed to hear Nora May herself speaking to me directly, her frail and beautiful hands reaching out to me in greeting and farewell, out of the shifting films of distance, the strange mists of time, separating her in late 1907 from myself in that winter of 1960–61. Later, in a more leisurely fashion, I would read and then re-read her little book, assimilating Nora May's distinctive and significant muse. I came to understand why Sterling, Smith, and others had thought of her so highly, with such wonder and esteem.

Meanwhile Clark Ashton Smith died in August 1961. A book of his writings that I had edited for Arkham House, *Poems in Prose*, appeared in 1965, and that led to my making another direct link to the California Romantics. I had already learned of Oscar Lewis, not the anthropologist but the literary historian, who had served for many years as the secretary for the Book Club of California. I contacted him, he responded, and I visited him at his home in San Francisco. This was in the early 1970s. I gave him a copy of *Poems in Prose* that I had inscribed to him on behalf of the deceased author. Certainly Oscar Lewis knew who Smith was, and had known of him much earlier in the century, before he became a distinguished and well-known historian of the American West. In his official capacity as the secretary for the Book Club of California he had known George Sterling, and had even met Ambrose Bierce, albeit with a certain trepidation, because of Bierce's reputation for being nasty (at least in print), when the latter had visited California for the last time during the summer and autumn of 1912.

As it turned out, Bierce as a strikingly handsome older man proved exceptionally gracious, charming, and witty, in short a perfectly civilized gentleman. It is with a certain wonder that I can say that I shook hands with someone who had shaken hands with California's Great Cham of Letters. A genial and generous man, Oscar Lewis in his own turn gave me a copy (graciously inscribed to me) of Bierce's monograph *Write It Right* (1909), as republished in a sumptuous edition for the Book Club of California in 1971. During our discussion he remarked that Bierce, a martinet about grammar and syntax, seemed to him rather "uptight" when it came to strict usage, and the Devil's Lexicographer would certainly seem so to us today.

I had moved to Northern California from Los Angeles in late 1965, and then in early 1966 from Auburn to San Francisco, where I would live during the period 1966 to June 1975, when I would move once again, but thence to Sacramento. The period 1965–75, the so-called hippie era, emerged as an especially fascinating time to be alive and well in the City of Saint Francis. A friend whom I had first met in Los Angeles (Pacific Palisades) through the science-fiction writer Fritz Leiber, Randal Everts Kirsch, had meanwhile begun his notable career of seeking out the surviving relatives of certain famous Californian and non-Californian poets and writers, particularly those in the genres of fantasy and science fiction. In late 1967 or early 1968 Randy contacted me, then living in San Francisco, to let me know that he had found Helen French Hunt, the surviving sister of Nora May French. She was then residing in South Pasadena and was the widow of Charles Hunt, an expatriate Englishman living in Pasadena, whom Helen had married in 1910 and who had just passed on during the early 1960s. Randy mentioned that she was not only an extraordinary individual but still quite beautiful as a woman in her mid-80s, definitely something worthy of notice. Her physical and other personal beauty I confirmed for myself when I met her in person sometime after first hearing of her from Randy. Somewhat later this fact made me realize that Helen as a young woman must have been as beautiful as her sister, or almost so.

At the time of my first meeting with Helen early in 1968, I was living at 50 Divisadero Street, sharing an apartment with several other friends. This was the bottom flat of the ostensibly two-flat building but with a basement flat underneath. The house itself was located in the area where Castro and Divisadero Streets run parallel to each other for several blocks. Divisadero to the north and Castro to the south make up a major north-south artery of an older part of San Francisco that lies at least several blocks immediately north of the Castro–Market area, and some distance west of Van Ness Avenue, and thus west of the main area that had suffered near total destruction in the earthquake and fire of April 1906.

As had become her habit after her sister's death, Helen would come to San Francisco to visit several times a year, first during the approximate period 1910–60 with her husband, and then later, obviously, without him. Randy had arranged a visit for the three of us; this took place either in February or in March, that is, in late winter or early spring of 1968. Randy, who had a car, picked Helen up at some small but nice hotel where she was staying downtown just a little south of Market Street. It was late morning when they arrived. They came to the apartment, which I luckily had to myself, the other roommates being at college or at work. The living room, simply but pleasantly furnished, lay at the back or eastern end of the flat, overlooking the back yards below. The large chamber had a coal-grate fireplace, and here we first became acquainted and socialized for an hour or two before we went out to lunch, Randy driving the three of us there and back. The socializing continued at lunch, and then on into the early afternoon, after which Randy drove Helen back to her hotel. In general, everything had gone quite well. I recall my being utterly thrilled at meeting Nora May French's only sister!

Helen was perhaps five foot six inches in height and had a slender but well-knit and elegant figure, dressed simply but quite well, including hat, coat, and handbag, displaying an understated good taste. It became apparent at once that she was not only a woman of great beauty, particularly for an older woman, but she was a person of great culture, considerable knowledge, and innate graciousness, able to discuss a wide variety of topics with taste and savoir-faire. Altogether she made great company, and her companionship and conversation turned out to be a delight. What more could one ask? During lunch, when I commented with playful admiration on how fit she seemed, she smiled pleasantly and confided that she exercised every day except when illness prevented. A Swedish doctor, her regular physician many years ago, had taught her a regimen of simple exercises—ones that she could easily do no matter where she found herself. She drank and ate with moderation and enjoyed alcoholic beverages on occasion, wine with meals, or cocktails with friends. Moreover, Helen had a keen sense of fun—in this she must have resembled her sister—and a slightly mocking but not off-putting sense of humor. What did we discuss? As expected on our first visit, we made much conversation about her now near-legendary sister. It was inevitable. Randy and I would pose apt questions or suitable topics about Nora May, and as Helen answered with skill and concision, the strangely beautiful world of an earlier San Francisco with attendant Bay Area came back to life, a world otherwise long since vanished. After lunch during our early afternoon visit back at the flat, Helen gave me the telephone number and address of her hotel, as well as her room number. Since Randy could not remain in the City for very long at that time, Helen and I arranged that we should meet later that same week, and at her hotel for another visit and lunch. She already had my telephone number and address. Because I did mundane work only part-time, I enjoyed considerable flexibility of schedule, and I would not have missed the chance of seeing her again, right away, for anything in the world!

We did indeed meet again later that week at Helen's hotel. We socialized again for an hour or so, then went out to a pleasant restaurant nearby for lunch, and afterwards returned to the hotel for another hour or so of socializing. Our first two visits established in general the paradigm for all our future visits, whether in San Francisco, Los Angeles, or elsewhere: several hours of socializing with wonderful conversation, a meal sometimes at noon but usually in the late afternoon or early evening at some suitable eatery often close at hand, or less often at some fancy place, as for example at an expensive old hotel in Sausalito north of San Francisco, followed by another session of socializing with stimulating conversation again. Often cocktails would precede the going out and eating, all very civilized and enjoyable, Helen often regaling us with amusing anecdotes. Her sister did not always become the main focus of our conversational exchanges, but the subject of Nora May and her poetry did in fact come up often and naturally.

Somewhat later than the first visit that the three of us managed to share, Randy either dropped off in person during one of his occasional visits to San Francisco, or mailed me, a photocopy of the photocopy he had made of the M.A. thesis that Judith Allen had written in 1963 for the English Department at Mills College. As things developed, this unique record of Nora May's life and writing provided some notable, even irreplaceable, assistance in compiling further information about the dead poet. To this day I remain extremely grateful to Randal Everts Kirsch for having introduced me to Helen, an introduction that led to what evolved into one of the best and most memorable friendships that I have ever enjoyed. Similarly, his giving me the photocopy of Judith Allen's M.A. thesis represented a very kind and generous act, a gift moreover that has clearly stood me in good stead in assembling the present volume.

Be that as it may, with or without Randy, Helen and I had established our own friendship, and over the years we would not only exchange visits in person but would also write letters back and forth to each other on occasion. Thanks to Randy, we had launched a great friendship together, and it would soon form a special joy to share Helen with other special friends whenever she came north from Los Angeles to San Francisco two or three times a year. The most special of these friends turned out to be Marvin Hiemstra and Lloyd Hansen, who lived then, and continue to live, in the City together. The fact that I am a poet who writes in traditional prosody did nothing to mar Helen's appreciation of my own work, or to hinder our burgeoning friendship. At the same time Helen remained resolutely open to new modes and currents in poetry and the other arts, as witness the depth and enthusiasm she came to bring to Marvin's own highly original and brilliant modern poetry, very different from what I sought to achieve.

Also, and a very nice bonus, this unexpected friendship led to one of the best personal poems included in the first series of *Songs and Sonnets Atlantean* (1971), "Thy Spirit Walks the Sea," inspired by her sister's memory, invoked for me so lovingly by Helen. I worked on the poem off and on between spring 1968 and winter 1968–69, and went down and back, on the good old Greyhound bus, at the end of that year to stay with friends overnight in Monterey. The next morning, the very last day of that year, 31 December 1968, my friends dropped me off at Point Lobos, where I dedicated the poem by reciting it aloud, and where I read or also recited from memory other poems appropriate to the occasion, not only the requisite memorial ones by Sterling and Smith, but especially a medley of suitable ones by Nora May herself. Later, after the friends picked me up around noon and brought me back first to their apartment for lunch and then to the bus station in Monterey, I returned to San Francisco that afternoon, at once profoundly moved and refreshed by my poetical adventure at Point Lobos. Earlier I had also sent a copy of "Thy Spirit Walks the Sea" to Helen, and it obtained both her approval and her appreciation.

As an instance of her being open to things both old and modern, but that were in fact new specifically to her, I cite a particular one that comes immediately to mind. Helen especially appreciated the Germanic tradition, symphonic or otherwise, in classical music, whether German or Austrian in origin, whether from the period of Johannes Sebastian Bach, or even earlier, or from the period of the First Vienna School, starting with Haydn, Mozart, and Beethoven, and ending with the powerful and opulent symphonies of Brahms, Bruckner, and Mahler. However, in the mid-1960s, somewhat before my meeting with Helen, I had discovered one further creator following these last three composers, as personally associated with all of them in various degrees and continuing their particular tradition, but also managing to innovate within that tradition in a vital and unexpected way, taking hints from Debussy, Schoenberg, and Hindemith. This was Franz Schmidt (1874–1939), the Austrian symphonist little known outside the Germanophone world in those days, but commonly regarded in that world as bringing to an end the First Vienna School in a completely worthwhile and epochal manner.

For a long time all that I knew by this composer was the marvelously beautiful and majestic "Intermezzo" from his first opera *Notre-Dame*, a German verismo work based on Victor Hugo's famous novel, as performed by the Berlin Philharmonic conducted by Herbert von Karajan, and recorded on Deutsche Grammophon along with other operatic intermezzi. Later I came to know the four epochal symphonies and the "colossal" organ works by this composer, but the initial impact of that unique "Intermezzo" has never faded, and I shared the piece eagerly with other friends, first with Marvin Hiemstra, quite an advanced musician and pianist, and then soon thereafter with Helen herself.

Her reaction did not disappoint me. Helen understood the grandeur and implications of the piece at once, a piece that seems to sum up in its five or ten minutes an entire century of the musical romanticism that had preceded it. I had sent her a copy of the twelve-inch long-playing record containing it, and she promptly played it on such high-fidelity equipment as she possessed. Helen confided in the note that she sent back to me that "the music seems to expand the mind," and that each time she played it the morceau seemed to expand the mind yet further and further.

On another occasion, somewhat before I separated from my wife, I almost succeeded in having Helen meet Genevieve Sully of Auburn, the close friend and inspiratrix of Clark Ashton Smith. Genevieve certainly knew Nora May's *Poems*, Clark probably having introduced her to the little book. Helen and Genevieve shared almost the same age and came of the same generation. I telephoned back and forth between the City and Auburn, as Helen had come up to San Francisco; I had a friend standing by to drive Helen and myself to Auburn and then back, and everything seemed auspicious for this momentous event—but then at the last minute it all fell through, all our careful arrangements and other preparations. Needless to say, we all felt a considerable disappointment, to put it mildly. The meeting of two such exceptional women, of two such exceptional minds and aesthetic sensibilities, would have made for quite a memorable occasion. Alas, "The might-have-been, the never-more-to-be," to quote that poignant line from Sterling's poetic narrative "Duandon." As I recall, Genevieve did not live very much longer, and Helen followed her in a few years. It is with a certain wonder and profound appreciation that I can claim to have known two such extraordinary women friends.

For the five years of our relationship, no matter where I went, no matter what curious adventures I had—marriage, separation, divorce, my first poetry readings and performances, my very own first book (1971), my first trip to England (where I lived for the first half of 1972), then my return from England, first to the East Coast, and then finally to the West Coast—I had Helen's friendship, encouragement, and patronage to help and inspire me. And if at times I did something egregiously stupid and out of line, she never failed to let me know how she felt, albeit in an unfailingly tactful manner. Since I have always lived frugally, and since I have operated almost always without abundant funds, Helen would send me from time to time a check for some small but useful sum of money, a check that would often arrive at a most opportune moment. These little sums, arriving when my own funds had reached some perilous low point, made a real difference in my life, and I used them only for essential things.

What words can one speak in praise of a friend like that? Such friends are few and far between at best, and all the more to be thanked, to be treasured, whether at the time of their kindnesses, or in retrospect, in memoriam. The present memoir, however inadequate, I proffer with deep gratitude and solemn piety to the manes of Helen French Hunt, friend nonpareil.

THEOSOPHY, HELEN FRENCH HUNT, NORA MAY FRENCH

As a codicil to the memoir of Helen French Hunt, I should add this note about a special subject or interest that Helen and I shared, or rather that Helen shared with me, a subject that one could call speculative thought, depending on how one might classify something that seemingly partakes of religious or philosophical thought or both. I mention it here because it has direct implications for Nora May French's poetry as well as her inner life. Both Helen and Nora had grown up in the late nineteenth century and had matured in the early twentieth century, a period when theosophy, promulgated by Helena Blavatsky, or Yelena Petrovna Blavatskaya, born Helena Hahn (1831–1891), started by her at New York City in 1875, gained a considerable vogue among educated people of progressive or advanced thinking throughout the European and neo-European world. Other spiritual movements also flourished at the same time, in addition to the established religions.

Helen herself belonged for some considerable time to the branch of Blavatskayan theosophy that had set itself up as the Theosophical Society in Altadena, not far from Pasadena. The society has published for many years the bimonthly magazine *Sunrise*. For much of the five years of our friendship Helen gave me a gift subscription (which she renewed every year) to this fine magazine, which I faithfully read, and the articles of which Helen and I would mention or discuss in our exchange of letters. One could see how the general direction of theosophy's thinking fitted in with the Platonism and Neoplatonism beloved of poets and other creative people, not to mention the mysticism common to many cultures and religions of both east and west.

The word *theosophy* means knowledge or wisdom of things divine. Theosophy itself, as defined since the later nineteenth century, means the doctrines and beliefs of the modern school or sect begun by Mme. Blavatsky, a school or sect that follows, for the most part, Buddhistic or Brahmanic theories, particularly in teaching a pantheistic evolution and the doctrine of reincarnation. There are hints and suggestions of theosophical thinking here and there in the poetical output of Nora May French. One salient example springs out at us from "Vivisection." "We saw Grief's sudden knife / Strip through the pleasant flesh of soul-disguise—" Such a passage presents immediate affinities with theosophical thinking or intuition. Much of what might seem transcendental or metaphysical in Nora May's poetry could very well be theosophical in origin, granted that these three terms denote modes of thought or feeling that have much in common with one another.

Note the quotation with which Pamela Herr ends her biographical sketch of Nora May French (the current one available on the Internet, 2006): "'It was her personal nearness to the great unseen,' Mary Austin tried to explain the tragedy. 'To her the film between life and the hereafter was so thin that it seemed a little thing to break through it.'" This astute citation correlates beautifully with this passage from Mary Rudge's tribute to Nora May:

and / so thin the veil between the worlds, easy to step through,—

Both passages correlate even more beautifully with the basic epistemological premise on which Mary Harriott Norris has founded her fine, atmospheric, and once well-known short novel *The Veil*, subtitled *A Fantasy*, published by Richard C. Badger of Boston in 1907, oddly enough late in the same year in which Nora May herself died. This romance, a work of speculative fiction if there ever was one, is drenched in the theosophical thinking so fashionable in the late nineteenth and early twentieth centuries. Since that initial period, such thinking has entrenched itself so deeply in our everyday consciousness, and has such obvious affinities with the mysticism common to many cultures and religions of both east and west, that we tend to forget just how much of Californian culture owes to theosophy, and that includes the poetry of Nora May French.

Tributes

GENERAL NOTE

Henry Anderson Lafler, during mid-1915, considered publishing a small book of tributes in verse and in prose to the memory of Nora May French, but he never did so. The present appendix of tributes, in the form of poems in verse for the most part, fulfills that intention and moreover demonstrates that, whether in the past or continuing into the present, an informal community of poets has existed in support and admiration of her poetic art—not only the California poets of her own time and immediately following but also those of today. A special word, however, is needed on behalf of the tributes by Lafler himself, at once her lover and her mentor, but with whom she broke off relations some two and a half months before her death in mid-November 1907. Lafler has now the unenviable reputation of being (inter alia) a "notorious womanizer."

It would be therefore easy to assume that, whatever else it was to Lafler, his love affair with Nora May could not have meant the same thing to him that it meant to her. Lafler apparently was romancing other women simultaneously while still married to his first wife and professing his love to Nora May. However, a profound examination of his chief tribute, "The Pearl," reveals that, if nothing else, Lafler must have loved Nora May very much, indeed. In this magical poem of "marvellous beauty" (to quote from the editor's note that heads the poem's appearance in *Sunset* for October 1908), Lafler has captured the wonder that he felt at the special quality of Nora May's persona, as well as the profound sense of loss that he experienced at her death by suicide, and has transformed them into a remarkable symbolic elegy.

Sources

Untitled ("Unleft the sun warms his forgotten hands"), by Henry Anderson Lafler. Transcription of a poem by Lafler, written in his hand on a photograph of Rodin's statue, "The Eternal Idol," and dated November 1907. From the John Lafler Family Papers.

Sonnet ("False, strangely false, am I beyond your guess") by Henry Anderson Lafler. Unpublished sonnet; from a typescript in the John Lafler Family Papers.

Sonnet ("All loveliness is sorrow evermore") by Henry Anderson Lafler. Unpublished sonnet; from a typescript in the John Lafler Family Papers.

"The Pearl," by Henry Anderson Lafler, *Sunset* (October 1908).

"Nora May French," by George Sterling, *A Wine of Wizardry and Other Poems* (San Francisco: A. M. Robertson, 1909).

"The Ashes in the Sea," by George Sterling, *The House of Orchids and Other Poems* (San Francisco: A. M. Robertson, 1911).

"Nora May French: In Memoriam," by Louise Gebhard Cann, *Ainslee's* (November 1919).

"To Nora May French," by Clark Ashton Smith, *Ebony and Crystal* ([Auburn, CA: Clark Ashton Smith, 1922]).

"Thy Spirit Walks the Sea," by Donald Sidney-Fryer, *Songs and Sonnets Atlantean* (Sauk City, WI: Arkham House, 1971).

". . . to secret places," by Dorothy Jesse Beagle, *Nora May French: Her Poems* (Oakland: Star Rover House, 1986).

"For Nora May in Paradise," by Mary Rudge, an original poem expressly revised and completed for this volume.

"Nora May," by Alan Gullette, an original poem expressly written for this volume.

"In Memoriam Nora May French," by Valerie Beatts, an original poem expressly written for this volume.

"Quicksilver," "November, " "The Poet Replies," "Dear Critic, Dear Abstraction," by Do Gentry, all original poems expressly written for this volume.

"The Poet with Us: Nora May French," by Marvin R. Hiemstra, an original poem expressly written for this volume.

[Untitled]

Henry Anderson Lafler

Unleft the sun warms his forgotten hands—
Unknown the chill stone grinds his hurlèd knees:
His soul is swung above the Pleiades,
And, wonderfully stilled, he understands
God! . . . . Earth's haggard deserts of blown sands
Are naught, and naught the grey and weary seas.
One moment between two infinities
His flesh is loosed of the insatiate bands.

[Sonnet]

Henry Anderson Lafler

False, strangely false, am I beyond your guess,
Girl, who so charms away my long despair
With warm enchantment of your breasts and hair.
The paler brows of feignèd mistresses
Allure, and I, adrift in dreams, caress,
Beyond your lips, those visioned lips and fair,
You are not you, but, sweet and unaware,
The mould of high-imagined loveliness.

And once, a night of windy moon and cloud,
By conjury of vast desire She came
And crept into your body, as a shroud—
Dying upon your lips I cried, "'Tis she."—
Whose mortal beauty, vanished of the flame,
Was blown, a little dust, upon the sea.

[Sonnet]

Henry Anderson Lafler

"Et in mare illi sepulchrum fiebant."

All loveliness is sorrow evermore,
And perfect beauty but a thrust of pain.
Never I see the silver of the rain,
Or blue of hills beyond a distant shore,
Or sweet, small flowers upon the forest floor,
Or hear lost waters wistfully complaint,
But makes my infinite desire again,
And Memory sets ajar her golden door.

All still, white dawns are tremulous with her,
And twilight is her hall and sacristy.
In shining nights of heaven her ferments stir,
But ah, dear Christ! this slays me utterly—
A sudden vision of the changeless sea,
The immortal purple of her sepulcher.

The Pearl

Henry Anderson Lafler

In the water pale and clear—
Wan, clear water of the sea—
Laving lands the sun is near
Whither soft and ceaselessly—
From the spicy islands—blow—
From the fragrant forests—go
Little winds to charm the sea,
Drifting perfumes to the bay
Where the red-sailed pearl-boats lay—
In a year remote and far,
On a gold and purple day,
When the iris-armored gar,
Breaking water in his play,
Glittered like a silver bar,
And the long, white, curving strand
Hitherside the sweet, green land
Was an ivory scimitar
On a cloak from Samarcand—
Purple with a green-gold band—
Bare brown divers found for me
(In the caverns of the sea—
In the water pale and clear—
Wan, clear water of the sea)
A great pearl and mystery.

* * *

I can well remember yet
How with shining bodies wet
They came slowly and reverently
Bearing that great pearl to me.

They had found it where a wall
Cold and coral is and tall
Round whose gleaming parapet
Monstrous surges foam and fret,
And whose glimmering base is set
In a vast and dim sea-hall—
In a twilight violet—
In a sepulchre of ships—
On the flowerless ocean-floor,
Stiller than a dead girl's lips.

Night by night beneath the moon—
Night by night beneath the stars—
Listening the water's croon
Round the tropic river-bars,
My sad pearl I gazed upon—
Beautiful it was and wan—
All the sweet, warm nights it shone;

And from out its hidden heart
Faintest music seemed to start,
And sad, ghostly murmurings
Of strange sea-enchanted things
Dwelling in dim halls apart;

* * *

Murmurings of the galleon
Plunged to shadow from the sun,
And the dreams that drowned men dream
In their sleep but just begun—
Whispers of the brown seaweed
That the untilled levels breed,
Ever swaying in the stream
Like a dancer in a dream;
And the ships that, captainless,
Moored where with black marble mix
Porphyry and sardonyx,
Rot in deep forgetfulness;

And all delicate fair things
Such as some dim-dreaming pool
Hidden from sea-murmurings—
Round and clear and still and cool
In a hollow beautiful—
Marred not save with shadowings
Of the gulls' wide-spreading wings—
Stirred not save when, least of life,
Frail sea-things, ephemeral
In their dim and secret strife
Make a grain of sand to fall,
Opal-colored, fine and small.

Whiter than the whitest star—
Brighter in the bright moonlight
Than a girl's white eyelids are,

Kissed by lover in the night,
Was my pearl unto my sight,
Whispering ever unto me
The eternal mystery
Of the blue, unsceptered sea.

Lost forever is the pearl,
Staked and lost in high carouse
Where the naked dancers whirl
In the hell-hot gaming house;
And they bore it over-sea,
And they bore it over-land
For a great queen's treasury—
For a warm white woman's hand—
Far, oh far, from where the strand,
White as women's souls may be,
Takes beneath the fading moon
Cool caresses of the sea.

And its heart remembers not—
Well I know it hath forgot—
Where the flaring tapers shine
'Mid the fumes of yellow wine
And where clouded-warm it rests
'Twixt a woman's bared breasts—
All forgot, that pearl of mine,
The cool silence under sea,
Wonder, dream, and mystery
Whereof long it whispered me.

Nay, it murmurs now no more
How upon the coral floor
Of the still, empurpled bay
Dimmest, bluest shadows sped
Of the galleys overhead—
Of the silver fish that fled.
Of the golden fish that lay
Quiet all the azure day.

Lost forever is the pearl—
Staked and lost in one wild night
Where the painted-dancers whirl
In a seeming mad delight.
I shall see it nevermore
Or its glory gaze upon
In the moonlight warm and wan
Of the island's scented night;
But a memory I keep,
Dear as dreams and soft as sleep,
Of its magic murmurings
Of the sea's most secret things,
Sweet and holy, treasured deep.

Sad are mine the silver dreams
As I walk in ways apart,
And the crystal memory
Of its lost and silent heart—
Heart that knew the golden gleams
And the blueness of the streams

And the mystic word, meseems,
Lips of loveliness impart.

Tremulous and silver clear,
Where the warm, soft sea-wind blew,
Listening my heart did hear
All things marvelous and dear,
Magical and sweet. I knew,
There, the white sea-marge beside,
All its soul, before it died.

Nora May French

George Sterling

I saw the shaken stars of midnight stir,
      And winds that sought the morning bore to me
      The thunder where the legions of the sea
Are shattered on her stormy sepulcher,
And pondering on bitter things that were,
      On cruelties the mindless Fates decree,
      I felt some shadow of her mystery—
The loneliness and mystery of her.

The waves that break on undiscovered strands,
      The winds that die on seas that bear no sail,
      Stars that the deaf, eternal skies annul,
Were not so lonely as was she. Our hands
      We reach to thee from Time—without avail,
      O spirit mighty and inscrutable!

The Ashes in the Sea

N. M. F.

George Sterling

Whither, with blue and pleading eyes,—
    Whither, with cheeks that held the light
Of winter's dawn in cloudless skies,
    Evadne, was thy flight?

Such as a sister's was thy brow;
    Thy hair seemed fallen from the moon—
Part of its radiance, as now,
    Of shifting tide and dune.

Did Autumn's grieving lure thee hence,
    Or silence ultimate beguile?
Ever our things of consequence
    Awakened but thy smile.

Is it with thee that ocean takes
    A stranger sorrow to its tone?
With thee the star of evening wakes
    More beautiful, more lone?

For wave and hill and sky betray
    A subtle tinge and touch of thee;
Thy shadow lingers in the day,
    Thy voice in winds to be.

Beauty—hast thou discovered her
      By deeper seas no moons control?
What stars have magic now to stir
      Thy swift and wilful soul?

Or may thy heart no more forget
      The grievous world that once was home,
That here, where love awaits thee yet,
      Thou seemest yet to roam?

For most, far-wandering, I guess
      Thy witchery on the haunted mind,
In valleys of thy loneliness,
      Made clean with ocean's wind.

And most thy presence here seems told,
      A waif of elemental deeps,
When, at its vigils unconsoled,
      Some night of winter weeps.

Nora May French: In Memoriam

Louise Gebhard Cann

I am not bitter for myself alone;
    But for those others who go stumbling out
    Before their time, those fervid ones devout
Whose jewels unto men are naught but stone.
Their days defeated slacken in a groan
    And meet the dark, knowing the maskèd rout
    Was rendered vain by life's envenomed knout;
Doubting that time may for their blood atone.

Not for myself shed I the heavy tear;
    But for my sister gasping in the dust,
Her meaning vague, her self-appointed bier
    Crying her, "Offal!" She who carried song,
    Gave it by pang to breathe its holy trust
    And heard it silenced by the cursing throng.

To Nora May French

Clark Ashton Smith

Importunate, the lion-throated sea,
Blind with the mounting foam of winter, mourns
To cliffs where cling the wrenched and labored roots
Of cypresses, and blossoms granite-grown
Lose in the gale their tattered petals, cast
On bleak, tumultous cauldrons of the tide,
Where fell thine molten ashes. **** Past the bay,
The morning dunes a dust of marble seem—
Wrought from primeval fanes to Beauty reared,
And shattered by some vandal Titan's mace
To more than time's own ruin. Woods of pine,
Above the dunes in Gothic gloom recede,
And climb the ridge that arches to the north
Long as a lolling dragon's chine. The gulls,
Like ashen leaves far off upon the wind,
Flutter above the broad and smouldering sea,
That lightens with the fire-white foam: But thou,
Of whom the sea is urn and sepulcher,
Who hast thereof a blown tumultuous sleep,
And stormy peace in gulfs implacable—
What carest thou if Beauty loiter there,
Clad with the crystal noon? What carest thou
If sharp and sudden balsams of the pine
Mingle for her in the air's bright thurible
With keener fragrance proffered by the deep

From riven gulfs resounding? *** Knowest thou
What solemn shores of crocus-colored light,
Reared by the sunset in its realm of change,
Will mock the dream-lost isles that sirens ward,
And charm the icy emerald of the seas
To unabiding iris? Knowest thou
The waxing of the wan December foam—
A thunder-cloven veil that climbs and falls
Upon the cliffs forevermore?

                          Thou art still
As they that sleep in the eldest pyramid—
Or mounded with Mesopotamia
And immemorial deserts! Thou hast part
In the wordless, dumb conspiracy of death—
Silence wherein the warrior kings accord,
And all the wrangling seers! If thy voice
In any wise return, and word of thee,
It is a lost, incognizable sigh,
Upon the wind's oblivious woe, or blown,
Antiphonal, from wave to plangent wave,
In the vast unhuman sorrow of the main,
On tides that lave the city-laden shores
Of lands wherein the eternal vanities
Are served at many altars; tides that wash
Lemuria's unfathomable walls,
And idly sway the weed-involvèd oars
At wharves of lost Atlantis; tides that rise
From coral-coffered bones of all the drowned,
And sunless tombs of pearl that krakens guard.

II.

As none shall roam the sad Leucadian rock,
Above the sea's immitigable moan,
But in his heart a song that Sappho sang,
And flame-like murmur of the muted lyres
That time has not extinguished, and the cry
Of nightingales two thousand years ago,
Shall mix with those remorseful chords that break
To endless foam and thunder; and he learn
The unsleeping woe that lives in Mytilene
Till wave and deep are dumb with ice, and rime
Has paled the rose for ever—even thus,
Daughter of Sappho, passion-souled and fair,
Whose face the lutes of Lesbos would have sung
And white Erinna followed—even thus,
The western wave is eloquent of thee,
And half the wine-like fragrance of the foam
Is attar of thy spirit, and the pines
From breasts of darkling, melancholy green,
Release remembered echoes of thy song
To airs importunate. No wraith of fog,
Twice-ghostly with the Hecatean moon,
Nor rack of blown, phantasmal spume shall rise,
But I will dream thy spirit walks the sea,
Unpacified with Lethe. Thou art grown
A part of all sad beauty, and my soul
Hath found thy buried sorrow in its own,
Inseparable forever. Moons that pass
Immaculate, to solemn pyres of snow,

And meres whereon the broken lotus dies,
Are kin to thee, as wine-lipped autumn is,
With suns of swift irreparable change,
And lucid evenings eager-starred. Of thee
The pearlèd fountains tell, and winds that take
In one white swirl the petals of the plum,
And leave the branches lonely. Royal blooms
Of the magnolia, pale as beauty's brow,
And foam-white myrtles, and the fiery, bright
Pome-granate flow'rs, will subtly speak of thee
While spring hath speech and meaning. Music hath
Her fugitive and uncommanded chords,
That thrill with tremors of thy mystery,
Or turn the void thy fleeing soul hath left
To murmurs inenarrable, that hold
Epiphanies of blind, conceiveless vision,
And things we dare not know, and dare not dream.

Note: Nora May French, the most gifted poet of her sex that America has produced, died by her own hand at Carmel in 1907. Her ashes were strewn into the sea from Point Lobos.

"Thy Spirit Walks the Sea"

Dedicated to Nora May French, in memoriam.

Donald Sidney-Fryer

"What shifting films of distance fold you, blind you,
    This windy eve of dreams, I cannot tell.
I know they grope through some strange mist to find you,
    My hands that give you Greeting and Farewell."
        Nora May French, Ave atque Vale.

Standing upon this lyric promontory
Which rises up beside the western sea,
We muse on Phyllis and her Sapphic glory:
Since that same time when you but seemed to flee
And in these waves they cast your ashes free,
Now more than half a hundred years have passed:
Beyond this world, its impure grief and glee,
You hold a greater world . . . the ocean's vast . . .
With whose untrammeled realms your spirit shall outlast:

Within what sunken colonnades and gardens do you roam,
Amid what palaces of some deep Atlantean past? . . .
Whose regal ways you have returned to claim once more as home:

And have you found —beyond this planet's barriers and bars—
Those greater spheres and realms . . . deep in the Ocean Sea of stars?

        Point Lobos: 31 December 1968

[Nora May French]

. . . to secret places

Dorothy Jesse Beagle

Tall and beautiful
Innately, powerfully feminine,
Yet,
It was her wistful undercurrent,
Her soft, 'escape through death,'
That was a Siren's Song
To her fellow poets and authors.

She was their ethereal
Golden Girl . . .
    lonely walks
    to secret places
    was she graced with
    special knowledge
    of the soul
    and its seeking?

1986

For Nora May in Paradise

Mary Rudge

Me! Come! My dazzled face
In such a shining place!
(Emily Dickinson, XXVI)

'06 earthquake. Beautiful city charred remains
Earth cracked open, blood red sky, chaos,
fire, smoke. Under concrete agony of slow dying.
Survivors, after, for their short lives—and
so thin the veil between worlds, easy to step
through,—(some), wore lockets, rings,
with bead of poison, for less painful death.

When earth cracked open, something new
was being born, people rose phoenix-like from
quick-pitched tents, rewrote a city,
rebuilt concrete towers, streets, charm.

Something new was being born, new come
to all this, slight being of light, a golden girl
of youth and life, bringing poems,
walking along the wood-planked streets.
(Where some, crushed, died, death's flame
set its ember in her heart).

Nora May French from LA, to San Francisco,
then, Carmel, city hum and singing forest.

Little crusader,* dreamer,* worker,*
first of all wed to her art.
From San Francisco, to Carmel,
lived as a green nymph in a tent, a sun gleam
spirit among thick dark trees shade,
near Mary Austin's tree house wikiup,
on Torres Street, before it had a name,

for big bonfires on the beach,
laughing, shouting fun songs,
lusty sensual eating of oysters, abalone,
with friends, soon-to-be-famous Bohemians.

With poems unborn, By her own hand, she died,
still wed to only art. Died by Society's mores
of her time. The Dead don't say why,
keep secrets. Seedling curled within her,†
(don't say who, don't say it's so) home-made
death, in her tent, swallowing cyanide.

"So brave," said Carrie Sterling,
"She played the game. . . ."
 A golden hairpin in the tent floor crack.
Heart break quake. They gave her ashes
to the waves, burned her clothes among the
trees. Soul disappeared, elusive as air.
We grasp whatever poem we can
to feel her presence, light, bright, green-gold eyes,
thick gold hair, that living girl of love.

Nora May, almost cult-like her memory grew.
She will be young forever now, some die
(Jack London gone like smoke) some grow old—
Harry Lafler, Joaquin Miller, Ambrose Bierce,
Gelett Burgess, those she knew then,
Ina Coolbrith, at 80, California's Poet Laureate
with circle formed around her.

George Sterling turned the ring on his own finger,
heavy, silver, capsule of poison in the hinged stone.
Death should be simple, quick, sweet on the tongue,
for poets who die, even for earthquake survivors,
and no matter now how many years he lived,
would come his turn.

> My Paradise, the fame,
> that they pronounce my name.
> (Emily Dickinson, XXVI)

*refer to Nora May's poems: "Vivisection," poem titled "VI," and her story "Diary of a Telephone Girl" published in *Saturday Evening Post*.

†refer to Nora May's poem "Best-Loved."

Author's note: I began this poem in the 1980s after visiting and interviewing the young second Mrs. James Hopper, at her home in Carmel (Hopper had built a house on the site where Nora May had lived and died), with Mrs. Bradley Buckminster (of Artists Embassy International), her friend, also of Carmel. Poem revised/completed 2006.

Nora May

Alan Gullette

I. The Promise Broken

Standing upon this headland by the sea
We watch the waves that waft eternally
And peer back to one moment in the Night
When one heartbroken soul put out the light—
Enamored of love, lovers, and the need to be—
And so deprived us of her maturity.

What stranger blossoms may yet have bloomed—
Or common ones of uncommon perfume—
What rare harvest would she reap in rime
If she did bide her time?

If her golden tresses had turned sterling grey,
What wise things might her pen still write—
What insight into the lot of man—
What vision into the depths of night—
What solemn song would she enchant us sing along
(Yea, even though we leave the common throng),
Or song of light come skipping from her tongue?
If she had only lingered on . . .

But captured here in haunted Time,
Her life a flicker in the Now—
A tragedy we seek to make sublime
With broken rime and knotted brow . . .

II. The Huntress Hunted

You pranced into the wood in doeskin wrapt,
Eyes glittering like torches in the night,
Hair wild as the underbrush and bracken
Splashed with the sun's true light.

If men could view you other than a peach,
Nor a flower in the midst of May—
Chaste and so chased, as if a thing to purchase . . .

Hounded by men high of rank and stature
Gone mad as the Hatter, the March Hare highly hopping,
Appealing mid peals of laughter, chasing after
With heavy thumping, lumbering through the ancient woods,
Your heart seeking—running deeper into thickets, leaping,
A doe there with eyes of fear, heart stopping;
Surrounded by hunters everywhere, heart breaking.

As Cupid sent a legion in his stead,
Too many arrows pierced her lonely heart.
With quivers empty, suitors staring, start:
Their prize—the doe Diana—lying dead!

III. Witness

Standing yet upon this silent hill—
Though waves crash ever on the raging sea—
We witness in the throes of her death
Birth pangs of the Overwoman, unborn still.

2006

For Nora May French

Val Beatts

The sprightly love you captured on the page
Whereon you wrote, "We dare be brave at last!"*
Proved painfully prophetic in an age
When friends accepted suicide, aghast

Perhaps, at loss of friends, but not the deed
Itself, so stunning and so tragic when
Invoked and carried through by those who bleed
Unseen, unheard, from heart or head in pain.

Did your pain blossom when your head hit stone?
Or was it that despair which lovers feel
Who stare at ashes of the love they've known–
"Discordant they, or else forever still."†

You wrote the Truth that all who love must find:
It's to the future that Love is most blind!

September 27, 2006

---

*From Nora May French, "You"
†From Nora May French, "After-Knowledge"

Quicksilver

Do Gentry

> "As for thy heart, it runs from me, it is Quicksilver, it does not concern me greatly."
> —Nora May French, "Think Not, O Lilias"

The heart is a silken rope, coiled and knotted on the deck
of the Dutchman's ship that never reaches port.
A silver spoon tapping the side of an empty absinthe glass.
The murmur of women stitching a quilt embroidered with poppies.

To measure it is to catch the laughter of fools in a sieve.

The heart is an abandoned house
with walls the color of cinnabar and a roof of gray slate.
A pond where the night heron fishes amidst dusk's monochrome.
A tentative transliteration of the sea's variable script along the shore.

It does not concern me greatly.

It is pathetic: trembling,
the way the hand's shadow trembles,
poised above the almond-scented page,
the instant before the pen
falls
like a dagger
upon the
penultimate
word.

November

Do Gentry

"We will disagree violently on the subject of wind . . . "
—Nora May French to Henry Anderson Lafler, 22 August 1905

And so we talk of other things.

The sea: a charismatic speaking in tongues (you tell me)
surely, no (I say): a circle of toothless gossips stitching a winding-sheet.

The lighthouse you compare to a flickering votive.

In return, I say nothing of the foghorn's futile warnings,
but recount the local legend of a sunken galleon,
a sea-chest washed ashore spilling ill-omened treasure.

November, I insist (glancing inland) is a shadow caught in amber.
You disagree, and speak of softly tarnished brass, then digress
by way of persimmons to straw-scented rain.

As we climb towards the point, the silence thickens.

A single cypress struggles up from the cliff
into the brunt of late October wind—
the tree you once described as
clinging and *bending*—
barely holding on.

The Poet Replies

Do Gentry

" . . . the little string of your letters which sums up my knowledge of you . . . "
—Nora May French to Henry Anderson Lafler, 10 August 1905

A twig trembling with the weight of yellow leaves—
small gold hands, each hand grasping a golden pen,
and each pen moving like the needle of a seismograph
across a scrolling grid. A silken thread reeled out
as one loses oneself in a maze.
A garland of snowflakes cut from foolscap.

Now, the high-wire artist steps out onto blackness,
without a net: the wire invisible, as if nothing
kept her aloft—except the held breath of the crowd.

Yesterday's letter contained a treatise on imaginary numbers—
today's explores the delicate relations between
numerator and denominator / subject and predicate—
tomorrow's will surely be composed of equations
through which mathematical operators walk
like ghosts pacing a newly haunted house.

The ribbon tied around a box of roses?
Or a trail of bread crumbs dropped along the path?
No. Let me try once more.

Your letters
are a poor merchant's abacus
strung with pearls.

Dear Critic, Dear Abstraction

Do Gentry

"... which brings me to the interesting fact of the critic."
—Nora May French to Henry Anderson Lafler,
22 August 1905

Come, Harry, let's go for a walk.
I'll show you night-blooming cereus
and field-owl's clover, and teach you
to tell time by the corrosive laughter of crows.

I pole my heart-shaped craft into the current
and steer by a runaway star—
a fire opal, barely visible
on the farthest edge of the Mariner's Compass.

My instrument, I confess, is strangely strung
and strangely tuned, my music now April-green,
now onyx—no one will hear it for a hundred years.
(My preference for odd-numbered days? I was born with it.)

Come, Harry, now that you've opened the box
and the genii of song have escaped—what will you do?
My birthstone's amber—my creature: a butterfly
with spun-steel wings—my simple calling: words.

The Poet with Us: Nora May French

Marvin R. Hiemstra

"The leaf that falls to the ground a thousand miles away touches your life."
—Daniel Quinn

Nora May French and Humankind do not see eye to eye.
The poet rejoices to see an ivory and pink wild morning
glory open in the first ray of California sun.
Humankind sees border patrols in flawlessly pressed uniforms.

The poet waits patiently for an angle and a light just perfect
to see the iridescent violet-green back of a swallow in flight.
Humankind soars over continents to spy an infraction
of a decree purposefully crafted to be unclear.

The poet learns patience from Great Blue Heron who waits
for the bounty of necessity to appear at his feet.
Humankind strikes blindly at anything or everything.

Nora May French and Humankind do not see eye to eye.
A child of the universe—the poet loves far beyond the moment.
Humankind wantonly rejects all, but how can it reject a poet's child?

Humankind does not love Nora May French.
Humankind, dubious adjunct of Creation In Toto, loathes
Nora May's Sun Illuminated Unabridged Bliss Manuscript.

Nora May French loves Creation In Toto:
    every supple, profound blade of grass
    every butterfly wing abandoned in an artist's first dream
every second of clear perception exalted.

George Sterling listens carefully to his heart writing
"The Ashes in the Sea: Nora May French."
He understands that a spirit so loved by Nature
like Nora May is alive still in Creation's jubilant flow—

For wave and hill and sky betray
    A subtle tinge and touch of thee;
Thy shadow lingers in the day,
    Thy voice in winds to be.

Nora May French loves Creation In Toto:
Creation In Toto loves Nora May French.
Humankind is definitely not. Study to be Humantrue.
Rush to meet Nora May French aglow and loving in her poems!

Index of Titles

After-Knowledge 132
Along the Track 158
Answered 130
At the End 166
Ave atque Vale 165
Be Silent, Love 133
"Bells from Over the Hills Sound Sweet" 146
Best-Loved 77
Between Two Rains 79
By the Hospital 81
By Moonlight 154
Change 136
Chapel, The 108
Constant Ones, The 93
Down the Trail 144
A Dream-Love 155
Dusk 104
Garden of Dolores, The 129
Garden, The 109
Growth 135
How Ends the Day? 138
In Camp 86
In Empty Courts 143
In Town 148
Indifference 131
Instinct 94
Just a Dog 102
Little Memories, The 141
Lost Chimneys, The 95
Message, The 80
Mirage 103
The Mission Graves 157
A Misty Morning 150

Moods	149
Mourner, The	164
Music in the Pavilion	84
My Maid of Dreams	83
My Nook	139
Noon	152
Nymph, The	87
"Oh, Dryad Thoughts"	82
One Day	156
Outer Gate, The	75
Panther Woman, The	98
Pass By	142
Place of Dreams, A	159
Poppies	100
Poppy Field, The	99
Rain	76
Rebuke	85
Rose, The	78
San Francisco, New Year's, 1907	96
Spanish Girl, The	105
Stranger, The	92
Suicide, The	161
Think Not, O Lilias	160
"To Rosy Buds . . . ."	162
Two Songs	151
Two Spendthrift Kings	134
Vine, The	107
Vivisection	91
When Plaintively and Near the Cricket Sings	140
Wistaria	137
Yesterday	163
You	101
Your Beautiful Passing	153

Index of First Lines

A jagged crown they topped the town,	95
Across my thought has trailed your beautiful passing,	153
Ah, happier he who gains not	155
All elfish woodland things that Fancy broods—	101
As down I bent with eager lips	86
Ay, pluck a jonquil when the May's a-wing!	78
Be silent, love. I will not have you speak;	133
Because my love has wave and foam for speech,	164
Beloved, have I turned indeed so cold?	136
Beyond the tangled poppies lies a lake;	99
Break camp, the dawn is here!	144
By man forgotten,	157
Earth's parchèd lips	104
Faces that throng—and stare and come and go—	84
From forest paths we turned us, nymphs, new-made,	87
Here will we drink content, comrade of mine—	159
His love is warm and constant as the sun,	143
I face the tranquil day with tranquil eyes—	98
I see upon the desert's yellow rim,	103
I twine you, little trellis, close and fond,	135
Is this the world I knew? Beneath the day	154
It gathers where the moody sky is bending;	165
It is a silver space between two rains;	79
It was a joy whose stem I did not break—	77
Life said: "My house is thine with all its store;	75
Low-arched above me as I moved the hollowed air was clear;	150
Mind said, "Pass by.	142
My thoughts of you . . . although I strain and sigh	141
Now all my thoughts were crisped and thinned	163
Now evening comes. Now stirs my discontent . . .	140
Now foliaged darkness of low hills is kissed	83
Oh, Dryad thoughts of lovely yesterday! —	82
Oh, half way up the hill it was, where one might sit leaf-hidden,	139
Oh, when the afternoon is long and hazy,	146

Said the Old Year to the New: "They will never welcome you 96
She sat so quiet day by day, ... 92
So many times in those dark days, ... 102
So might it brush my cheek with errant wings, ... 80
Sweet grasses, tasseled, bent and tall; 149
The blue wistaria hangs with bloom 137
The brook flowed through a bending arch of leaves— 152
The garden of Dolores! Here she walked. 129
The levels where the trail began 156
The long street where the people go— 148
The moon crept in and found her dead, ... 130
The rain was grey before it fell, ... 76
The tortured river-banks, the toiling piers— 85
The tossing trees had every flag unfurled 93
The track has led me out beyond the town 158
The vanished women of my race, ... 108
There is a thread from you to me? 131
These tawny sheaves, this fragrant land, ... 134
They planted lilies where they might, ... 109
To Reason with the praise of one I go 94
To rosy buds in orchards of the spring, ... 162
To screen this depth of shade that sleeps 107
Tremblingly and spent I ran and fell, ... 166
We saw unpitying skill 91
We wandered where the violets bloom, beside the sunlit stream. 138
Where saffron poppy-petals curl apart, ... 100
Who goes to meet the windy night 81
You found my soul an untried instrument. 132
You love the chant of green, ... 151

www.ingramcontent.com/pod-product-compliance
Lightning Source LLC
Chambersburg PA
CBHW070641160426
43194CB00009B/1528